Fifty Hikes

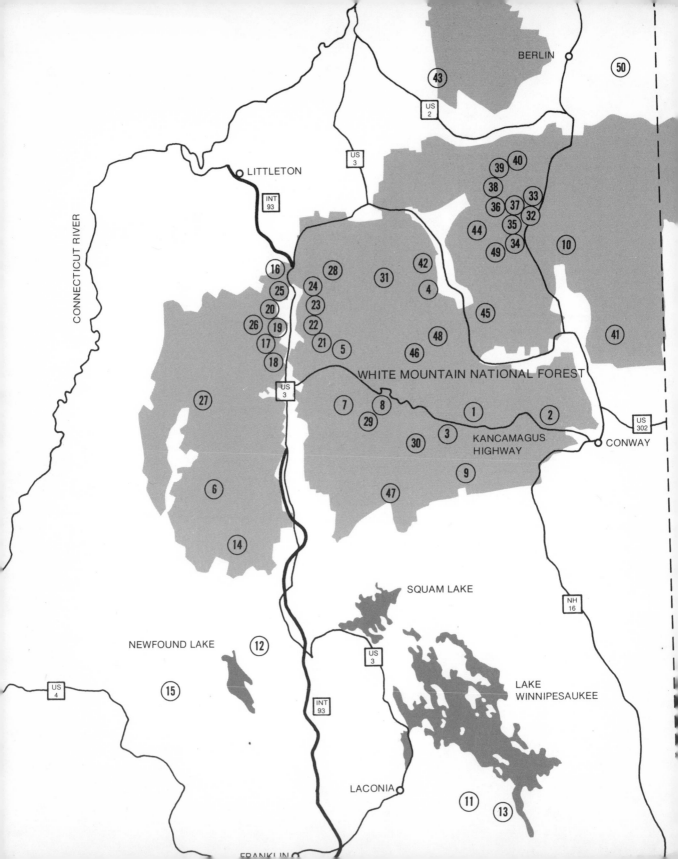

Daniel Doan

Fifty Hikes

Walks, Day Hikes, and Backpacking Trips
in New Hampshire's White Mountains

New Hampshire Publishing Company
Somersworth

Acknowledgments

During most of these excursions, and many others, I was hiking with Dr. Claud W. Sharps. I would like to express my appreciation to this former AMC hutman for his help, companionship, and experience in the more remote regions of the White Mountains. Also, I am grateful to Kurt Kuss for hiking with me on several of the climbs, and to James H. Rogers of the U.S. Forest Service.

I would also like to thank Frank Donegan for his valuable assistance.

D.D.

First printing: 1973
Second printing: 1974
Third printing: 1975
Fourth printing: 1976

Standard Book Number: 0-912274-23-9
Library of Congress Catalog Card Number: 73-76396
© 1973 by Daniel Doan
Somersworth, New Hampshire 03878
Printed in the United States of America

Designed by David May

Contents

Introduction

These excursions into New Hampshire's White Mountains are intended to initiate the beginner and entertain the experienced hiker. There are forty-five day hikes and five overnight backpacking hikes. They are arranged from short to long and from gradual to steep. The first five hikes are suitable for family outings. Then there are five woods walks, five hikes in small mountains, and thirty hikes in and around the Franconia Range and the Presidential Range. The five backpacking hikes run from a weekend to a week. Some of the hikes loop around to their starting points, which are, of course, the places where you leave your car. Other hikes follow the same route up to their destinations and back.

Most of the hikes are within the central White Mountains. There are several that take you to lesser-known outlying summits. The corners of the hiking territory are: Mount Major (hike 13), southeast near Lake Winnipesaukee; Mount Cardigan (hike 15), southwest near Canaan; Mount Starr King (hike 43),

The author hiking on Mt. Lafayette

northwest in Jefferson; and Old Speck Mountain (hike 50), northeast at Grafton Notch, Maine. Within this area, the hikes take you up all the major peaks of the White Mountains. The map facing the title page shows clearly the location of each hike.

The White Mountain hiking season extends from May into October. Winter weather occurs early and late. Above treeline, you may encounter icy storms at any time, even during the season. June and July have their black flies and mosquitoes; you'll need insect repellant. To my mind, September is the best hiking month. The heat of July, the August haze, and the bugs are gone for the season. Cool air and clear blue skies offset the customary September storms.

The Trails

The hikes follow established, well-marked trails maintained by the U.S. Forest Service, the New Hampshire Division of Parks, the Appalachian Mountain Club (AMC), and various other clubs. Forty-five of the hikes are in the White Mountain National Forest or in nearby state reservations. Some of the

hikes begin on, or cross, land owned by lumber companies, by Dartmouth College, or other private property. On trails crossing boundaries between private land and the National Forest, the Forest Service posts small yellow signs at the boundaries. Any abuse of the privilege granted to hikers on this private land could result in No Trespassing signs.

The mountain trails change due to slides, washouts, new beaver ponds, trees downed by winds, and heavy use. On the other hand, some, like the Crawford Path, have hardly changed in more than a hundred years. When necessary, trails or sections of them are relocated. Access roads and parking places may be restricted or relocated. For latest information, check with the U.S. Forest Service, the Appalachian Mountain Club, or the New Hampshire Department of Resources and Economic Development. U.S. Geological Survey topographic quadrangle maps are available at many sporting goods stores and book stores, or from the U.S. Geological Survey. For addresses see page 13. (On each diagram map, the top represents North.)

Logging Roads

The descriptions of the hikes refer often to logging roads. Almost all of these are *old* logging roads and have become part of the new forests. They are not raw bulldozed cuts for heavy modern logging machines. Only the trails keep them open. The old roads were graded for horses and sleds; although plentifully strewn with rocks, they follow the slopes at gentle angles. Together with the former railroad grades along the valleys, these old logging roads provide the best walking in the mountains.

The present logging operations supervised by the U.S. Forest Service leave the trails in wooded corridors.

A fascinating former logging territory, and a splendid example of new forests on land once devastated by logging and fires, is the area known as the Pemigewasset "Wilderness," those mountains and valleys east of Lincoln drained by the East Branch of the Pemigewasset River. It's not really a wilderness any more; a network of trails connects with the main Wilderness Trail, which runs up the river from the Kancamagus Highway. Part of the White Mountain National Forest, the watershed includes the 18,460-acre Lincoln Woods Scenic Area. For a day hike into the Pemigewasset "Wilderness," see hike number 5; for backpacking, try hike number 48.

Distance, Walking Time, and Vertical Rise

Each hike description begins with the figures for distance, walking time, and vertical rise. These are gauges by which you can evaluate the hikes.

The times allow for leisurely climbing, which seems to me the only pleasant and sensible way, but they do not include rest periods, lunch breaks, view gazing, or bird watching. Young, hardy climbers may cut the times in half.

The vertical-rise figure tells you the approximate distance up. If you start at a 1,000-foot elevation and climb to a 2,500-foot summit, you may walk two miles or five, but your vertical rise is 1,500 feet. Sometimes you climb down into a valley and up again to a summit; your return trip will thus include some climbing, which is included in the total, or round-trip, vertical-rise figure. As a general rule, you can expect that the greater the vertical rise per mile, the more strenuous the climb.

The White Mountain National Forest

The State of New Hampshire had disposed of its public lands by the mid-1800s, and logging began in earnest after the Civil War. Men with axes felled trees throughout the north country—except in the White Mountain's most remote valleys, where the steep slopes presented transportation problems. The rivers were too shallow and rocky for log drives.

Because of this and other difficulties, the forests of red spruce, pine, hemlock, and cedar in the White Mountains remained standing until late in the era, and some were bypassed completely as lumbermen cut a swath from Maine to Minnesota.

Finally, railroads opened the valleys in the 1880s and 1890s, and much of the timber was cut by 1900. Logging continued through the First World War and even as late as the 1930s, but, long before the cutting was complete, forest fires had devastated large tracts of cut-over land.

Conservationists, led primarily by the Society for the Protection of New Hampshire Forests, came to the rescue of the White Mountains in the early 1900s. The federal government purchased areas for watershed protection under the Weeks Bill beginning in 1912. By 1971, the White Mountain National Forest had grown to 728,516 acres, 45,944 of which extend into Maine.

The land is managed by the U.S. Forest Service under directives based on "multiple use." Among these uses are timber production, watershed protection, recreation development, and wildlife protection. Nine Scenic Areas and the Great Gulf Wilderness on Mount Washington preserve a total of 34,108 acres of valleys, ponds, and mountains in their natural beauty.

Trees and Animals

The mountainsides are now covered by hardwood forests of beech, maple, yellow birch, and white birch, which took over after the destruction of the spruce. Evergreens remain predominant in the swamps.

The upper summits, from about 3,000 feet to treeline, are green spruce/fir forests interspersed with white birch and mountain ash.

You will meet no dangerous animal life. This is not rattlesnake country. Black bears and wildcats are shy. I recall only six bears in forty-five years of walking the mountains, and they were all going away fast when they became aware of me. I never saw a wildcat in the woods. Porcupines can be dangerous to an aggressive dog; otherwise they mind their own business. Even *Homo sapiens* seems gentler in the mountains.

White-tailed deer are forest denizens seldom seen in the higher mountains. Moose inhabit the Mahoosuc Range and certain other sections, occasionally. You'll probably see a beaver, and more ponds than beavers. Coons, skunks, foxes, and flying squirrels come out at night. You'll probably see a snowshoe rabbit flash quickly into cover. Red squirrels and chipmunks will chatter at you.

In the text I mention birds because I like to watch them, and trees, flowers, and plants because I like to look at them. Field books to identify these, and the animals, will increase your enjoyment. I also recommend hikes number 1 and 3, which follow Forest Service nature trails, as introductions to the life of the woods.

Clothing and Equipment

Careful consideration and selection of the clothing and equipment for your hikes are essential. Basic apparel includes a cotton shirt, walking pants or shorts, comfortable underwear, and hiking shoes worn over two pairs of socks. As long as the weather is good, this is all you'll need to wear. If you're day hiking, pack the rest of the equipment in a strong, waterproof knapsack—no equipment dangling from belt or straps; no bulging pockets. Here's what you'll need: heavy wool shirt, sweater, or insulated jacket; poncho or rain suit with hood; nylon parka or shell; hat; gloves; warm pants; matches and firestarter in a waterproof container; compass; map and guidebook; pocketknife with can opener and screwdriver (Girl Scouts have a nice light one); a quart of water in a canteen or other container;

lunch; and spare food for two meals.

If you're backpacking, you'll need everything on the day hiker's list and more. In addition to an aluminum packframe and waterproof nylon packbag, you'll want to take a tent, or at least a waterproof tarp; a hiker's gasoline stove, aluminum fuel bottle, cook kit, forks and spoons; a down-filled sleeping bag in a stuff sack; a foam pad to place under your sleeping bag at night; a small first-aid kit, including moleskin for foot blisters (no snakebite kit necessary); soap and a towel; a small flashlight, two candles, and extra matches in a waterproof container; a small hatchet or saw (optional); light nylon cord to lash your sleeping bag, tent, or tarp to your packframe; and meals for each day of the trip. Food should be light and easy to prepare. Include ready-to-eat food for lunches. Standard necessities can be found at your supermarket: oatmeal, sugar, dried milk, tea, salt, hardbreads, cheese, canned meats, dried soups, etc. At your backpacking shop choose freeze-dried foods for super-light nourishment.

Along the trail on Belknap Mountain

Equipment is no substitute for experience. Learning how to walk in the woods is more important than the best hiking boots money can buy. On the other hand, hiking in tennis sneakers is not recommended. Leather boots, six to eight inches high, with rubber lug soles and weighing no more than three pounds, are a good choice. Break them in completely before you commit your feet to a long hike in them. If you are in a hurry to do this, put on the boots over two pairs of wool socks and then stand in a tub of water. Go for a walk, and walk the boots dry. They'll be broken in. Heavy mountaineering boots are unnecessary for these hikes.

As for socks, one pair of light wool socks under one pair of heavy wool socks seems to be the best combination. Pants should be loose. Fishnet undershirts are great: they keep you cool, keep you warm, pad your back under a pack, and stop insects from biting through your outer T-shirt. Down-filled jackets are comfortable beyond dreams as long as they're dry, but, when they're wet, I wish I had on that warm-though-wet product, wool.

I like a floating-dial compass, because I can never remember which end of a needle points north. (Note: In the White Mountains your compass points about sixteen degrees west.) I also use plastic flask-shaped water bottles (one-pint size) instead of a canteen. Two pack easily and fit into a mountain pool to fill. I carry a small cup to fill them from trickles.

Because equipment for backpacking is so extensive, and the choice arouses such vehement contention, you may want to read a book on the subject and explore a shop or catalog that specializes in backpacking and mountaineering equipment. Whatever you finally decide to take, be sure to set everything up at home and try it out before heading into the mountains.

Rules and Regulations

All rules and guidelines for hikers in the White Mountains, both those of the Forest Service and those promoted by the Appalachian Mountain Club, have been developed to save the forest from its greatest enemy, fire, and to preserve the areas that are becoming more and more popular, especially those with delicate ecology near treeline and above in the alpine zone. The days of the roaring campfire and the woodsman's bough bed are over.

The rules apply mostly to campers and backpackers, rather than to day hikers. However, anyone who plans to cook lunch over a fire or on a portable stove, outside the officially maintained campgrounds along the highways, is required to have a campfire permit. Free permits for the season may be obtained from the U.S. Forest Service Supervisor in Laconia (see page 13) or from district forest rangers in Conway, Gorham, Plymouth, or Littleton.

The mountains and your fellow hikers deserve an uncluttered trail. No litter, no trash left behind. And no random elimination—to put it politely, copy the cat. No candy wrappers, no cans or aluminum envelopes or any of the slick packages our civilization provides us for throwing away. If you take them in, take them out again in your pack. The motto is: "Carry in and carry out!" And another: "Leave only your footsteps."

Huts and Shelters

In the White Mountains the Appalachian Mountain Club and the Forest Service maintain most of the trails and shelters. Open-front shelters of logs or boards face stone fireplaces. The Appalachian Mountain Club has built closed huts or lodges to serve hikers on its trail system.

Long a prime mover in this area, the AMC was founded in 1876 and had 16,000 members in 1972. It maintains 350 miles of trails, fifteen shelters, and eight mountain huts, three of them above treeline. In the huts, crews of college students provide meals and lodging for hikers during July and August; some of the huts are open from the middle of June into October. The Pinkham Notch Camp on NH 16 is open year-round to accommodate skiers and hikers, and it also serves as headquarters for the system of trails, shelters, and huts.

Physical Fitness

Good physical condition increases hiking pleasure. Without it, the more strenuous hikes are no pleasure at all, and there may be harm and danger.

If you wait until warm weather to get in shape, the arrangement of hikes in this book will break the news gently to your body that you're going to take it walking. Nobody has to be an athlete to succeed with hike number 1; Mount Washington is something else again. In preparation for the longer climbs in the high Franconias and Presidentials, I've included a few relatively easy hikes for each region. In the Franconia Region, they are numbers 16, 17, 18, 19 and 20. In the Presidentials, they are numbers 32, 33, 34, and 35.

Stamina developed for walking and climbing provides not only pleasure but an important safety margin in the mountains. It's a form of insurance you can take out yourself.

Safety

Almost every year, the mountains claim some hiker's life. Storms are sudden and fierce above treeline. Trails over the bare rocks, marked only by cairns and signs at the junctions, disappear in clouds and wind-driven rain, sleet, and snow. Electrical storms shoot down lightning that bounces from the rocks amid torrential rain.

Besides physical fitness, two precautions may help you survive these dangers. First, in the face of threatening weather forecasts, don't go mountain climbing, or go to some lesser peak or a woods trail. Second, in the face of gathering low clouds and wind at treeline, turn back. The woods and shelter are only a few steps behind you; ahead you will climb into increasingly thick fog and winds so strong you'll be unable to stand.

On many trails leading above treeline, a Forest Service sign will warn you of the dangers ahead. They aren't kidding, either; above treeline you're in hazardous territory. Perhaps this fact, along with the tremendous views and the thrill of being there on your own two feet, gives above-treeline hiking its excitement.

It's important to hike with a companion. (Two old friends hike best together; I've been lucky this way.) Stay together. This is a rule of every mountain clubber, experienced climber, and all officials delegated to find the lost or injured lone hiker.

Carry a compass. Carry a map

that you have studied so you know about the route and the trails. Be prepared to spend a night out in the woods or under a rock. This means carrying extra food, water, warm clothing, and waterproof outerwear in a knapsack.

And last of all—but so important it might be first—before you set out tell someone where you're going, and give an alternate place for bad weather. Then go there, one or the other, and enjoy yourself. The hike is supposed to be fun. No bitching: not about the trail, the weather, or the world. Leave that attitude back with "civilization" and your other troubles.

I wish you years and years of great hikes in the White Mountains of New Hampshire.

Addresses

Appalachian Mountain Club
5 Joy Street
Boston, Massachusetts 02108
or
Pinkham Notch Camp
Gorham, New Hampshire 03581

United States Forest Service
Supervisor's Office
719 Main Street
Laconia, New Hampshire 03246

New Hampshire Department of Resources and Economic Development
Concord, New Hampshire 03301

United States Geological Survey
Washington, D.C. 20242

Introductory Hikes

On Mt. Lafayette

At the White Mountain National Forest Information Center on the Kancamagus Highway, 12½ miles west of Conway, you'll find this ½-mile nature trail featuring twenty-nine stops keyed to a pamphlet available free at the trail's entrance. Don't avoid this walk because it seems to lack challenge; don't let the tourists dismay you. There is a wealth of information here for the hiker who truly wants to know the mountains.

Shortly beyond the sign directing you along the trail, you become aware of trees and their history in forests logged-off and grown again. You walk on an old railroad grade. The rails are gone, and only depressions in the earth mark the ties. But, in the 1880s, steam locomotives hauled flatcars loaded with millions of board feet of first-growth timber to mills in the lower valley.

Take your time and enjoy the trees. They are identified with their common and scientific names. You'll see not only familiar pine and spruce, but also larch, alder, black cherry,

White Birch

Rail 'n River Forest Trail

1. Rail 'n River Forest Trail

Distance (around the trail): ½ mile.
Walking time: depends on how much you look and learn.

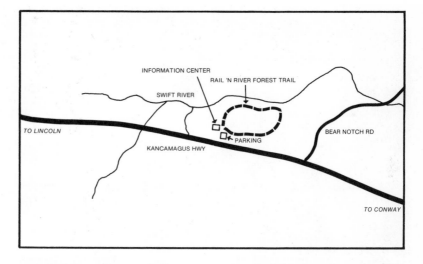

maple, white birch, poplar, and others. See rocks changing to soil that will support plants. Visit a swamp "garden" where you can study plants that thrive in wet ground and acid earth. Along the bank of the Swift River, you see stumps of alders and poplars gnawed down by beavers. Stop to look at the mountain named for the Indian chief, Passaconaway, who loved peace and, in 1627, organized seventeen tribes into a confederacy that, during his lifetime, lived compatibly with the white settlers. Learn how woods take over an abandoned field. Inspect forestry practices, conservation, and ecology preservation. All these will appear on future hikes, and you will recognize them. Knowledge of them will give a new meaning to the trails and mountains.

Rail 'n River Forest Trail is recommended for parents with youngsters who ask questions about the woods.

You can drive the Kancamagus Highway from either Lincoln or Conway. The distance to the Information Center is shorter west from Conway, about 12½ miles. From Lincoln, drive east

21½ miles over Kancamagus Pass. The sign to watch for— "White Mountain National Forest Information Center, Passaconaway"—hangs in front of a white cottage on the north side of the highway.

The cottage was built in 1810 on the flat land along the Swift River, known as Passaconaway Valley or Albany Intervale. In this mountain home, each night for thirty-nine years, Ruth Priscilla Colbath placed a lamp in a window, certain that her husband, Thomas, would come home. He had left the house for "a little while" in 1891. He returned three years after his wife's death at the age of eighty,

and found her grave in the nearby cemetery.

The restored cottage includes a Victorian country parlor and a beamed room containing mementos of the Colbaths and events of that era. In this old-time setting, you'll find modern information and Forest Service pamphlets about the White Mountains. Beside the cottage, a display room contains exhibits of stuffed animals, relics of lumbering days, maps, and posters dealing with Forest Service projects and the National Forest. Rail 'n River Forest Trail starts just east of the display room and terminates at the path behind it.

Boulder Loop Trail

2. Boulder Loop Trail

Distance (around the loop, including spur to ledges): 3¼ miles.
Walking time: 3 hours.
Vertical rise: 900 feet.

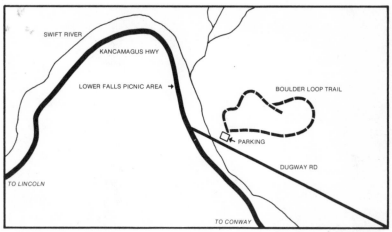

Like the Rail 'n River Forest Trail (hike number 1), the Boulder Loop Trail is for family walking and enjoyment, but it is a longer hike. Boulder Loop is keyed to sixteen stops (described in the Forest Service pamphlet available at the Information Center, Passaconaway). At each stop you learn about glaciers, rocks, and trees. Along the trail through hardwoods and evergreens, you see examples of soil formation and forest origins from the time of the glacier fifty thousand years ago: erosion, lichens and moss, elementary plants and trees, mature specimens of oak, spruce, fir, pine, hemlock, beech, maple, birch, ash, and various other trees native to the White Mountains.

You also see boulders, a rock slide, a brook, blowdowns from a northeast storm, fracturing granite, dry slopes with plants adapted to that sunny environment, contrasting cool-moist slopes, as well as birds and flowers in season.

Besides these, the trail takes you to a splendid outlook a

Hobblebush on Boulder Loop Trail

thousand feet above the Passaconaway Valley. A spur trail leads to ledges giving views from the highest elevation. You see Mount Chocorua's sharp peak and the bulky Mount Passaconaway beyond the nearer forested ridges. These lookoffs have the built-in dangers of all cliffs.

The trail should be considered a climb rather than a picnic jaunt. Suitable shoes and other clothing are necessary. A small knapsack frees your hands of lunch, camera, and jacket. Remember to use the pack for carrying out your empty soft-drink bottles and cans and cellophane wrappers.

To reach the trail, turn off NH 16 just west of Conway onto the Kancamagus Highway. Seven miles from Conway, turn right onto the Dugway Road and cross the covered bridge over the Swift River. Watch on the left for the parking area near the Covered Bridge Campground. From the west corner of the parking area, a sign directs you to the trail, which soon forks. Bear left for the first of the sixteen points of interest— a rock, smoothed by the ages, extending 100 feet along the trail and reaching up 30 feet. Lichens grow on it much as they did when they were the first plants on the bare rock of the world.

No more than an afternoon's jaunt, this popular short hike to Sabbaday Falls conveys an important message about the mountains. It suggests a new world to explore: one filled with outdoor sights, sounds, and sensations. It arouses a new or forgotten interest in the woods, the streams, and the miles of mountainous terrain around you.

The Sabbaday Brook Trail begins 16 miles west of Conway and NH 16 at a picnic area on the south side of the Kancamagus Highway. The graded path in a forest of maple, beech, and birch leads up to the base of the ledges through which the stream cuts its way.

A side trail, left, takes you down to the lower pool. There you may read the first of several Forest Service signs describing the geology of the falls. Stone steps and peeled-log railings ease the way up the ledges above the narrow flume that was formed by water wearing away a basalt dike in surrounding granite. From a deep pothole, the stream pours down into the

Upper Sabbaday Falls

Sabbaday Falls

3. Sabbaday Falls

Distance (picnic area to falls and back): 1 mile.
Walking time: ½ hour.
Vertical rise: 100 feet.

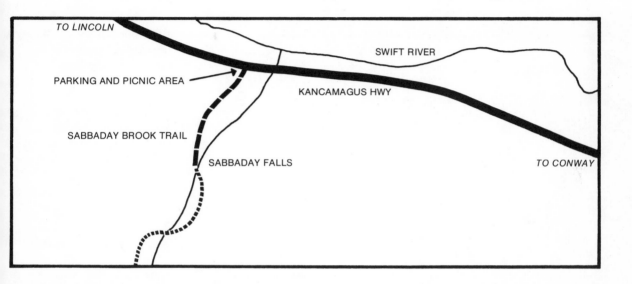

flume. The walkway returns to the Sabbaday Brook Trail above the falls. (The Sabbaday Brook Trail continues up the brook toward Mount Tripyramid.)

Approaching from Conway, you should treat yourself to a brief stop, 12½ miles along the Kancamagus Highway, at the White Mountain National Forest Information Center maintained by the Forest Service. (See hike number 1.)

Continuing west from the Information Center, you drive past the Forest Service's Passaconaway Campground, and, after 2½ miles, you cross the bridge spanning Sabbaday Brook. Turn left for parking and the trail to Sabbaday Falls.

Westward, the Kancamagus Highway rises steadily to Kancamagus Pass at 2,855 feet, then winds down to Lincoln and US 3 at North Woodstock, about 20 miles away. Signs mark other trails into the mountains north and south. (See hikes to Black Pond, number 5; Greeley Ponds, number 9; and Mount Hancock, number 46.) Before driving the highway, check your car's gas gauge; there are no service stations on the 34 miles between Conway and Lincoln, and, across the central 15 miles, no buildings.

The adventure of driving the highway persists despite its accepted use and the blacktop surface added in 1963. Before that, many tourists did not know of the completion of the gravel road's upper section, done in the summer of 1959, and uncertainty added spice. One tourist stopped near the Conway end to question an old lady rocking on her porch: "Does this road go across the mountains?" After a moment's thought she told him: "Well, a lot of cars pass by here and don't come back."

4. Kedron Flume

Distance (round trip): 1½ miles.
Walking time: 1¼ hours.
Vertical rise: 600 feet.

Crawford Notch is a pass through the mountains. For years it provided a route between the interior Connecticut River valley and the seacoast region. Discovered by hunters in the days when New Hampshire was a royal province, and explored by settlers following the Saco River after the Revolution, Crawford Notch became a teamsters' passage between sheer cliffs and steep forested slopes. The Notch is a state park now. A railroad and US 302 wind through it. But, a short distance into the woods, the mountains are still primitive and rugged.

For a brief hike into this mountain fastness, park your car at the Willey House site, 3 miles south of the Notch's gateway crags on US 302. A souvenir shop and lunch counter are nearby. The trail to Kedron Flume begins at the picnic tables above the shop.

Perhaps if the driving has been tedious and the kids squabbling, you can bribe your spouse into taking the children to the pond and wildlife exhibition on the opposite side of the highway.

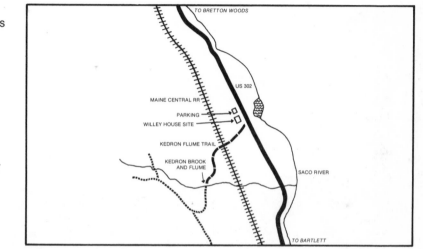

Whatever your arrangements, climb the Kedron Flume Trail to the railroad tracks near the site of the earth avalanche that wiped out the Willey family in the summer of 1826.

Across the tracks, the trail climbs the steep slope. Although graded and improved in places, angling left, it is a mountain trail. The soft stone gravel will roll underfoot. Watch your step, especially descending. The trail leads through beech woods toward spruces farther on. It bends around a shoulder and dips into a little ravine at Kedron Brook.

The stream pours down through a narrow sluice or flume in the rock and drops over the falls below the trail's crossing. Remember, rocks are slippery when wet. The wide outlook across the Notch's gash is to Mount Webster and its cliffs. Beyond, rise the Presidential Range's southern peaks and Mount Washington.

For ½ mile past the flume, the trail twists more steeply up among big spruces and rocks to its junction with the Ethan Pond Trail, a route into the Pemigewasset "Wilderness" past the Willey Range Trail up Mount Willey, which towers above Kedron Flume.

Kedron Flume

Black Pond

5. Black Pond

Distance (round trip): 6½ miles.
Walking time: 3½ hours.
Vertical rise: 480 feet.

With only 250 feet of upgrade in the first 2½ miles, the hike to Black Pond rates as an excellent "tryout" for new packs and boots. The route parallels the Pemigewasset River's East Branch on an abandoned railroad bed. The sparkling water and smooth boulders are typical of mountain streams large enough to scour out a valley during the annual ice-out spring freshet.

The East Branch and its tributaries drain a territory that extends from Franconia Range's eastern slopes to the western bastions of Crawford Notch, and to Mount Carrigain and Mount Hancock on the southeast. Bounded by the Kancamagus Highway on the south, and called the Pemigewasset "Wilderness," the valley is rich in the history of men who chopped trees and earned a hard living in the forests of spruce, which they devastated. Old loggers used to look back on those days with nostalgia and tell yarns about the lumber king, J. E. ("Ave") Henry, who hired them and made a fortune. Henry, a once-bare-foot, poor boy, became legendary for his toughness, man driving, determination, and parsimony. The territory he clear cut, which often went up in terrible forest fires, is now largely National Forest, but the Pemigewasset "Wilderness" could tell many tales of years gone by.

The East Branch flows fast and slow. It rises and falls rapidly. Logs were successfully driven down the Pemigewasset River to Lowell, Massachusetts, in the 1850s by a state-of-Mainer, N. G. Norcross, and his red-shirted Penobscot boys, sometimes known as Bangor Tigers. In the '90s when J. E. Henry began to cut the East Branch valley, he built driving dams to provide water flowage on which to float the logs downstream to his Lincoln mill. Many logs were too big for the river, so he built a railroad. It freed him from the temperamental water levels. The railroad grade now provides an easy path for hikers; it's known as the Wilderness Trail.

Black Pond lies in a hollow surrounded by forest, ¾ mile north of the Wilderness Trail.

Covering two and one-half acres, the pond measures as much as thirty-four feet in depth, indicating the pitch of the basin it fills. Because of a boggy crossing on the Black Pond Trail as it follows the outlet brook, you might expect a shallow, marshy pond, but you'll find instead a little mountain lake in which speckled trout swim. The rocky heights to the east are the ridges of Mount Bond. To the west is Mount Flume's pinnacle.

The Wilderness Trail, which will lead you to the branch trail for Black Pond, starts at a parking area along the Kancamagus Highway, 4¾ miles east of Lincoln. You will come to the parking area just before the concrete bridge over the East Branch. The trail follows the grade of the logging railroad, last used in 1948. There are no rails, and the ties are mostly rotted or buried, but watch out for an occasional broad-headed spike. The mixed second-growth woods are taking over after the chopping and fires. This is a popular trail into the Pemigewasset "Wilderness," because it joins trails

Black Pond

leading to the eastern extensions of the Franconia Range—Garfield Ridge and Zealand Ridge—and to Crawford Notch.

The Black Pond Trail branches left from the Wilderness Trail 2½ miles from the parking area and ¼ mile before Franconia Branch. For a short distance on a spur railroad grade, the trail passes a small pond, which once provided ice for the logging camps. About all that remains of the camps in the valley are rusty pieces of stoves, peavey spikes and hooks half-buried in the leaf mold, sled runners, and similar scrap iron. The occasional wild apple trees, which you'll come upon, sprouted from cores thrown out the cookshack doors.

Beyond the little pond and clearing, the trail enters the woods again, ascends and descends moderately uphill between crossings of the brook for about ¾ mile to Black Pond, where it ends.

If you approach quietly the light showing ahead through the trees, you may see two deer drinking in the water. If there is a hatch of flies, the trout will be dimpling the surface.

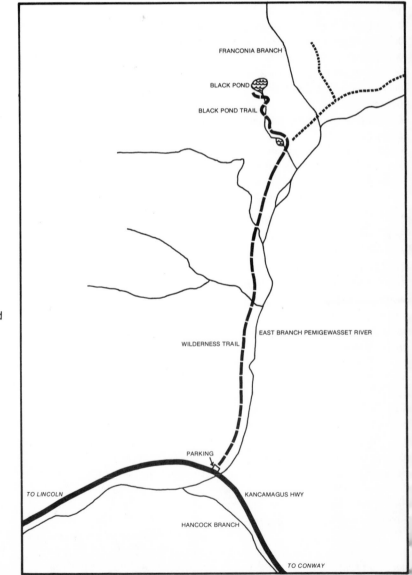

Black Pond

6. Three Ponds Trail

Distance (circle trip to Three Ponds and back): 3½ miles.
Walking time: 2 hours.
Vertical rise: 417 feet.

The hike to Three Ponds is a leg stretcher and fine for gaining woods experience. At a National Forest shelter near the ponds, hot dogs and beans can be cooked at an open fireplace. (Carry out your trash!) A weekend in June is a good time to visit this forest environment of boggy ponds and hardwoods and evergreens. Wild flowers, then abundant, will include pink lady's slipper, the little yellow flowers of clintonia, and carpets of Canada mayflower. White-throated sparrows give their haunting, north-country whistles. Joining in will be all the other returned birds.

But take plenty of fly dope. Blackflies will welcome you in June. Wear a hat. Tuck long pants into boots or socks.

Drive along NH 25 west from Plymouth and turn north through Rumney to the upper end of Stinson Lake. The trail leaves the road beyond the bridge over Sucker Brook, which is 6 miles from the Rumney village green. It soon passes, on the left, the eastern terminus of the Carr Mountain Trail and comes to a crossing of the brook. The trail

follows an easy grade up a wooded logging road, which is usually muddy in early summer. Much of the way, the brook is on your right, and you walk through a forest of maple, beech, and yellow birch.

The ponds are about 1¾ miles from the Stinson Lake road. You notice first the open-front shelter on a knoll to the trail's right. East of it is the smallest pond. The trail continues through the woods bordering the twelve-acre Middle Pond. Soon you come to a fork, where the Donkey Hill Cutoff bears right.

Keep left along Three Ponds Trail, which turns west between Middle and Upper Ponds. After a heavy rain, you hear the falls splashing down the west ridge into Upper Pond, from tiny Foxglove Pond. Upper Pond is interesting for its boggy ecology: waterbrush along the shore, evergreens, sheltered coves, and a slope of woods on the south with luxuriant wild flowers growing around old campsites of trout fishermen. Perhaps there'll be a swimming black duck suddenly beating from the water, possibly a mink or beaver if

Near Three Ponds

Three Ponds Trail

you wait silently on shore and listen to the thrushes.

Beyond Three Ponds, the trail ascends to the top of the ridge and leads on toward NH 118, which it reaches about 6½ miles from the Stinson Lake road. Parties with two cars might divide and start at both ends, swapping cars for the return drive.

Another variation could be a return via the Mount Kineo Trail. Take the Donkey Hill Cutoff to the Mount Kineo Trail, which you reach 1 mile from the ponds. Turn right (south) and follow the Mount Kineo Trail down along Brown Brook to the Stinson Lake road about ¾ mile from your starting point at the Three Ponds Trail.

Hikers with a two-car arrangement can try yet another variation. Follow the Donkey Hill Cutoff to the Mount Kineo Trail and turn left (north). This climb runs over Mount Kineo's upper shoulder—no trail to the summit— and descends to a spur of the Forest Service road in the Hubbard Brook Experimental Forest. You'll be about 4¼ miles from the ponds and 7 miles from US 3 at West Thornton.

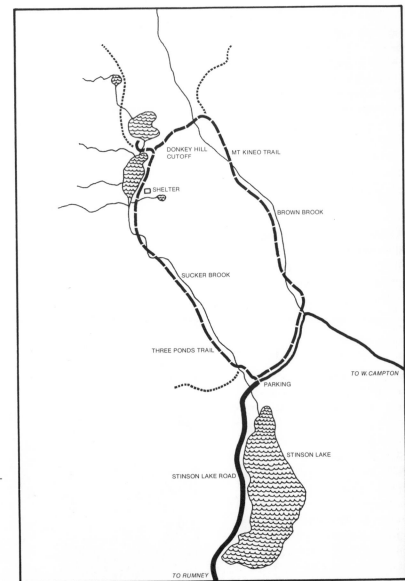

Three Ponds Trail

7. East Pond

Distance (Tripoli Road to East Pond and back): 3 miles.
Walking time: 2½ hours.
Vertical rise: 780 feet.

In its simple wooded setting, with Scar Ridge and Mount Osceola's West Peak in the background, East Pond resembles many small, high lakes, which nestle among the ridges and mountains surrounding the more impressive and famous peaks. Yet each is individual, a special goal for a hike. East Pond covers six and one-half acres. Much of the shore is lined with rocks, or gravel and sand. Dead trees standing in places testify to the flooding caused by beavers who build their dams at the outlet and inlet. The water is cool and clear; it reaches depths of as much as twenty-seven feet and provides shelter for speckled trout, which seem inclined to stay there.

Across Scar Ridge's spruce-grown slopes, green lines indicate the routes of old logging roads. Relics of those days—scrap iron and bolts—lie in the sand near the pond's outlet. A ditch guides the little brook to its drop-off into the valley.

In late September, berries of several mountain ash trees cluster in scarlet splashes above the shore and against the ridge, making a Christmas-

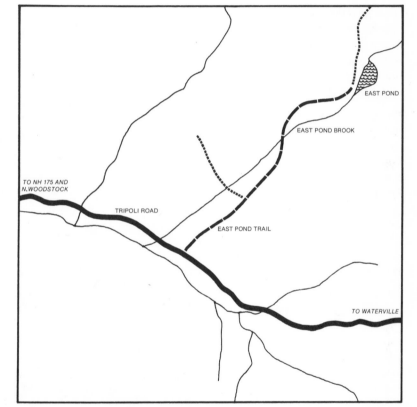

like display of green and red. In the spring, snow lingers in protected hollows. Hikers on Memorial Day may still find a melting drift near the outlet.

The East Pond Trail crosses Scar Ridge and 5 miles of woods between the Tripoli Road and the Kancamagus Highway.

The shortest route to the pond is from the Tripoli Road, which leads east off NH 175 about 3 miles south of the junction with US 3 near North Woodstock. The Tripoli Road is better known as the access to the Russell Pond Campground. It connects with the upper end of Waterville Valley and NH 49.

East Pond

Drive past the campground's entrance road on your left. About 5 miles from NH 175, watch on the left for the Forest Service signpost marking the start of the East Pond Trail.

Rising gradually through hardwoods, the trail climbs steadily for ½ mile. You pass a branch trail, leading across East Pond Brook to Little East Pond. The site of an old mill is on the right. Continue up the brook. In another ½ mile, you cross to the brook's west side and climb more steeply for the remaining ½ mile until the trail levels out at the pond.

For hikers continuing through to the Kancamagus Highway, the trail passes the south end of the pond and bears north over Scar Ridge. This is a climb of 1,000 feet above the pond in less than 1 mile, mostly along old logging routes. Of course, a hiker crossing between the two roads must arrange transportation at the end of his hike and must also consider whether the 3,600-foot elevation of the ridge is for him.

A resident of East Pond

East Pond

8. Greeley Ponds

Distance (round trip): 4 miles.
Walking time: 2½ hours.
Vertical rise: 400 feet.

The west shoulder of Mount Kancamagus and Mount Osceola's precipitous East Peak frame the two Greeley Ponds in a wild and mountainous setting. The northern or upper pond below Mad River Notch reflects the western cliffs; the lower pond narrows between boggy shores grown to spruce and fir.

As an official National Forest Scenic Area, 810 acres surrounding Greeley Ponds are preserved in their natural beauty. To this end, the Forest Service has taken down the old log shelter by the upper pond, because, paradoxically, it was too popular. Sanitation problems, fuel requirements for the fireplace, garbage and rubbish disposal, and campsites extemporized nearby all despoiled the scanty earth, the pure water, and the slow-growing trees. People were overwhelming the delicate environment they had come to enjoy. Greeley Ponds Scenic Area could no longer stand the wear and tear of more and more campers. So the Forest Service has asked overnighters to plan their trips elsewhere. Visit, but don't camp.

To reach the trail from Lincoln, drive the Kancamagus Highway east past the start of the Wilderness Trail (4¾ miles east of Lincoln) and over the concrete bridge above the Pemigewasset's East Branch. Follow the highway up Hancock Branch. Drive past the Forest Service's trail sign for East Pond on your right. About 1 mile farther (9½ miles from Lincoln), watch for a similar brown board on which engraved lettering directs you to Greeley Ponds.

The trail rises gradually as it crosses small brooks and the South Fork of Hancock Branch. It ascends to Mad River Notch, which is the height of land above

Greeley Pond

the ponds. The trail drops a short distance to the upper pond and follows under the cliffs along the west shore to a junction with the Mount Osceola Trail on the right. A spur trail, left, leads around the end of the pond to the former shelter site.

Straight ahead, the Greeley Ponds Trail continues past a spring on the right. In ½ mile it reaches the lower pond. (For about 2 more miles it leads west through fine evergreen woods and hardwoods, following the young Mad River, to Waterville Valley.)

The upper pond has an area of one and one-quarter acres and a maximum depth of twenty-seven feet. The lower pond averages three feet deep over its two acres. Beavers seem at home in both ponds. As a beaver swims past, his brown head leaves a wake like a toy power-boat. Alarmed, he whacks his tail on the water and dives immediately.

Greeley Ponds

You may want to return to eat your sandwiches by the upper pond. Spruces and pointed firs rise toward the cliff and reflect in the still water. Speckled trout break the surface to suck down hatching flies. Juncos and white-throated sparrows call from the trees. Cedar wax-wings flutter over the pond to catch bugs, then return to a tree branch alongshore and preen their glossy feathers. Swallows skim above the spruces or dip into the pond for an instant of a skimming arc after insects. Dragonflies patrol the airways.

For a bird's-eye view, climb up the steep Mount Osceola Trail as far as the ledges, about ½ mile. First, through the open spruce forest, you may notice a little-known profile to the southwest. From the rock face, the wide view centers at the tiny lake far below. Watch your step on the ledges. They are dangerous when wet or icy, and you'll want to return safely to the pond for final minutes close to an intrinsically wild harmony of water, rocks, and trees—before you return to your car by the same route you followed up.

A Note on Overuse

The increasing popularity of the mountains creates a problem faced by the Forest Service, by the Appalachian Mountain Club, by other mountain clubs, and, in fact, by all conservationists and all citizens: overuse.

Hikers, like all mankind, congregate, and so destroy the primitive environment they seek. On Mount Washington, Tuckerman Ravine camping had to be restricted to protect the trees, plants, and soil; they are responding. In the Franconia Range, Liberty Spring Shelter has been replaced by tent platforms. Campfire and camping regulations throughout the White Mountain National Forest are being extended to preserve both the forests and the areas above treeline.

Easy access to the mountains is certainly not the whole problem, but it may be part of it. The Kancamagus Highway accounts in some measure for the popularity of Greeley Ponds and the consequent overuse at the shelter. (You can still find recalcitrant old timers who think the cross-mountain road between Lincoln and Conway never should have been built.)

Especially in the eastern United States, the boundless spacious-ness, the frontier freedom, no longer exists. "Wilderness" is an unrealistic term, misunder-stood by many visitors to the White Mountains. A hike along the Wilderness Trail following the Pemigewasset's East Branch will convince anyone that "wilder-ness" is a misnomer.

With care and preservation, the mountains can be a continuing source of "wildness" in the deepest sense, of life force from the trees, moss, lichens, birds, and animals—but only if men control their own "wildness."

Greeley Ponds

The loop from Wonalancet over the Old Mast Road and Kelley Trail connects with other trails between NH 113A and the Kancamagus Highway. The area offers hikes and climbs of varied distances and destinations in the Sandwich Range—mountains that extend west from Mount Chocorua and include Mount Paugus, Mount Passaconaway, Sandwich Mountain, and others north of the Lakes Region.

A hike need not be a physical challenge. Woods walking provides the satisfactions of escape and seclusion as well as the pleasures of striding and breathing deeply. For these purposes, the Old Mast Road–Kelley Trail combination is ideal.

According to legend, the Old Mast Road was first cut through the primeval forest to haul out great masts for the British navy. The trail's ascent up even contours toward Paugus Pass, and the long stretches without a turn, would seem to bear out the legend. For contrast, the return route takes you scrambling down Cold Brook via the Kelley Trail.

Along the Old Mast Road

Old Mast Road and Kelley Trail

9. Old Mast Road and Kelley Trail

Distance (round trip): 5 miles.
Walking time: 3¼ hours.
Vertical rise: 1,000 feet.

Drive to Wonalancet on NH 113A from Sandwich or Tamworth. Turn north at the corner in the meadow. After about ½ mile, park on the road's left edge opposite a trail sign at the corner of a field by a dirt road.

Walk along the dirt road to the woods and across a brook to an opening used for yarding logs. (From the right of this opening, the Kelley Trail crosses a brook and goes up the right bank. This will be your return route.)

The Old Mast Road bears left into the woods, and, under Mount Wonalancet's slope, climbs through the forest of beech and yellow birch. During a warm, damp August, many mushroom varieties appear almost overnight. There are both edible and inedible varieties, and, of course, some very poisonous ones. Among the toxic varieties are the deadly amanita, both the yellow type and the white species known as the Destroying Angel. Fragrant orange chanterelle, smelling of apricots when warmed in your hand, shaped like a little inverted twisted saucer on a stem, is a gourmet's delight. But, unless you are an expert on the various

species, don't take chances by eating any of them.

Birds along the trail are typical of the deep woods, such as thrushes, although a scarlet tanager sometimes flits and calls among the high branches, or a fluttering redstart flashes among smaller trees.

The rugged, older, yellow birches have a reddish-brown-gray bark, scaly and furrowed, as though a different species from the younger trees with their pale yellow bark that peels across the trunks in ribbons and layers. Their leaves resemble those of the white birches sometimes growing near.

Easily distinguished are the smooth, gray, beech trunks common along the trail, which they shade by extending their muscular branches almost horizontally. The branches end in slender twigs and light green leaves; the delicacy seems to belie their strength. The burrs enclosing the triangular nuts begin to open in late August, to the delight of squirrels and bluejays.

After 2½ miles, the Old Mast Road terminates at a junction

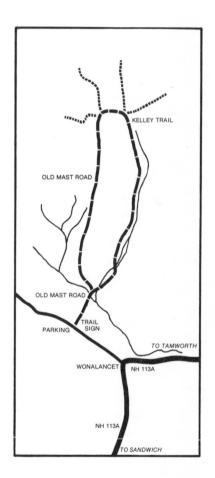

on the height of land named Paugus Pass. Continuing north, descending, rough, is the Square Ledge Trail. Left, or west, the Walden Trail leads up Mount Passaconaway. Right, or east, the Lawrence Trail crosses the pass and climbs Mount Paugus. The Lawrence Trail also leads to the Kelley Trail, which is your return route for this hike.

Turn right (east) on the Lawrence Trail and follow it ½ mile to the Kelley Trail. At their junction, the Lawrence Trail continues its rough and steep ascent east up Mount Paugus. To the left (north) the Oliverian Brook Trail leads, after about 4½ miles through wet ground along Oliverian Brook, to the Kancamagus Highway. For your return to Wonalancet, turn right (south) and follow the Kelley Trail into the ravine of Cold Brook.

Here the trail descends over rocks and past falls and through gloomy, cool woods of big spruces. A ledge split again and again looks like the stone work of an expert mason. There may be deer tracks on the miniature sand bars, maybe a winter wren on a mossy log, trilling like a coloratura canary. Lush woodland ferns grow from dark humus and curve over rocks. Hobblebush blossoms are white in early summer—they turn to green berries later, then red. Graceful, gray-green lichens thrive on ledges.

Lower down in the valley, the Kelley Trail crosses to the east bank of Cold Brook. You then walk ¼ mile, recross to the west bank, and emerge from a logging road at the junction with the Old Mast Road. Turn left across the opening and follow the dirt road back to your car.

Old Mast Road and Kelley Trail

10. Wildcat River-Bog Brook Loop

Distance (around the loop): 6½ miles.
Walking time: 4 hours.
Vertical rise: 700 feet.

This hike follows a circuit north up the Wildcat River (some maps call it Wildcat Brook) Trail, then east along the Wild River Trail, and returns via Bog Brook Trail. The attractions are streams, beaver ponds, and woods, woods, woods.

Beavers as conservationists specialize in water storage. The ponds behind their dams of poles, brush, and mud are gathering places for birds, animals, and insects. The boggy shores are wetlands where sphagnum moss and pitcher plants grow. The moss can flourish, seemingly rootless, even in open water and forms an absorbent mat as vegetation begins to take over the shallows. Farther back from shore under evergreens, the delicate pink-white twinflowers grow from beds of green moss. On Bog Brook Trail, if you have stopped smoking for the summer to improve your hiking wind, you'll smell the almond perfume of the twinflowers.

In the beaver ponds, water drowns the trees growing on flooded ground, and the dead trunks provide homes for birds. A pair of wood ducks nest in a hollow stub. Flickers—yellow under the wings—drill out nesting holes with their strong beaks. A pileated woodpecker, black, white, and red-crested, and big as a crow, scatters chips as he hammers for grubs. Kingbirds nest on the top platform of a high broken stub and keep eyes alert to drive off a cruising hawk. Chickadees lay eggs inside the white bark that surrounds inner rotted wood of birches. Swallows take over old nesting holes of downy woodpeckers.

Snowshoe hares hide in the tall swale grass and eat sprouts growing from old beaver cuttings. White in winter and brown in summer, the hares are preyed upon by the weasel who follows the same color changes. Bobcats won't be seen, and probably not a bear, for they both avoid humans. The white-tailed deer leave V-shaped tracks at night on muddy shores. Moose? Perhaps.

The hike starts at the end of the Carter Notch Road north of Jackson. Leave NH 16 on NH 16A over the covered bridge. Beyond a hotel and the village stores in Jackson, a right turn takes you up NH 16B on the west side of Wildcat River. After about 2 miles, NH 16B turns right, across the river. You continue straight ahead on the Carter Notch Road. Its upper dirt section may be impassable to ordinary cars. A logging road forks left. The dirt road bears right to a turnaround, 5½ miles from the covered bridge. Here the trail enters the woods, and you start walking.

The Wildcat River Trail leaves the east side of the turnaround, soon crosses two small brooks, and in ½ mile reaches the Wildcat River, which in this upper valley is a small stream that can usually be stepped across from rock to rock. The trail climbs the steep opposite bank to a left turn on an old logging road grown to grass and bushes. This shortly brings you to the Bog Brook Trail, which branches uphill to the right. (You will return by way of the Bog Brook Trail.)

For now, continue straight ahead on the Wildcat River Trail. It follows the easy logging road through a clearing with views of the mountains at Carter Notch. Up the pleasant wooded valley,

A beaver pond

sometimes bearing away from the clear stream on the left, the trail crosses Bog Brook and continues north along Wildcat River as it dwindles to a mountain brook.

After you've been walking for about two hours, this first section of the hike's triangular loop meets the second section, the Wild River Trail, which now joins from the right. (The Wildcat River Trail continues to Carter Notch and the AMC hut, 1¾ miles farther and 1,000 feet higher.)

Turn to the east, right, on the Wild River Trail, which takes you, in about 1 mile, to the Bog Brook Trail along the upper reaches of that brook as it comes down from Perkins Notch into the spruce swamp near the junction. Bog Brook Trail is the return, or third, section of the triangular loop. (The Wild River Trail continues east, over hardwood ridges to Perkins Notch and the watershed of the Wild River—8 miles to the Wild River Campground.)

The Bog Brook Trail branches right. Watch for a sign in the

Wildcat River—Bog Brook Loop

evergreens at the junction. Then look for blazes and arrows as you cross a beaver dam to the old trail, which may require care to follow through a flooded area. The trail winds south and southwest to another crossing of Bog Brook. Beavers have been active on this stream for many years. Their insatiable instinct to hold back flowing water has left old dams, meadows, and new ponds along the trail. After the final crossing, the trail angles away into the woods along a former logging road. Wet ground is bypassed; otherwise the trail follows this logging road down to the Wildcat River Trail. Turn left, retracing your earlier route across Wildcat River to the turn-around and the parked car, with your memories of a remote little corner in the White Mountains.

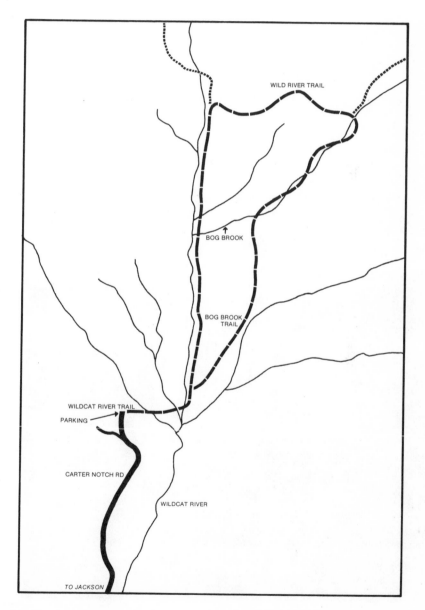

WILD RIVER TRAIL

BOG BROOK

BOG BROOK TRAIL

WILDCAT RIVER TRAIL

PARKING

CARTER NOTCH RD.

WILDCAT RIVER

TO JACKSON

Wildcat River-Bog Brook Loop

A short climb to the lookout tower atop Belknap Mountain opens a view across Lake Winnipesaukee's blue water and many islands. The Ossipee Mountains rise beyond in impressive array, green ridge upon green ridge forming a long single mountain from this distance. To the left, fifty miles away and unmistakable in spring and fall when it alone displays snow, Mount Washington appears distant yet splendid. Nearer and somewhat in line, peaks of the central and west Sandwich Range group themselves beyond the far end of Lake Winnipesaukee. Still more to the left and again distant, the line of rocky Franconia Range is dominated by Mount Lafayette. Foothills around Mount Moosilauke fill in the panorama continuing west. On a sunny day the passing high clouds shift light and shadows upon the lake and mountains.

Of the four summits in this small, circular range south of Lake Winnipesaukee, Belknap Mountain is the highest, although perhaps not so well known as Mount Gunstock with its ski

Lake Winnipesaukee from Belknap

Belknap Mountain

11. Belknap Mountain

Distance (round trip): 1½ miles.
Walking time: 1¼ hours.
Vertical rise: 740 feet.

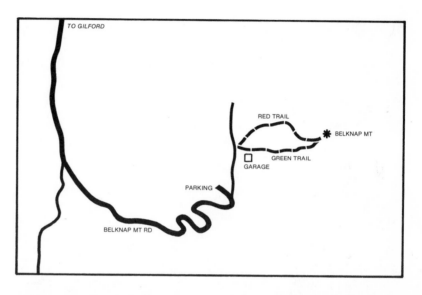

TO GILFORD

RED TRAIL

BELKNAP MT

GREEN TRAIL

GARAGE

PARKING

BELKNAP MT RD

area of the same name. Mount Gunstock and Mount Rowe are usually climbed by trails from this ski area, where information is available. The fourth summit, Piper Mountain, is a bare ridge to the south. Belknap Mountain offers not only the highest summit, 2,384 feet, but also a mountain drive to a picnic area.

Turn off NH 11A at Gilford and proceed south through the village. The road, in a residential area, makes a sharp left turn and climbs to the top of a ridge; it then turns right, and continues south under the mountain slopes to the Belknap Mountain Road, which forks left about 2 miles from Gilford. This blacktop road leads into a steep valley, winds upward, changes to gravel, resorts to switchbacks, and ends at a level parking area.

For the trails to the summit, walk uphill along the continuation of the road and past a small garage. A wide service route on the right goes up near the telephone and TV cable lines. This is the Green Trail marked with green paint blazes. More pleasing to hikers is the Red Trail beginning on the right a few yards along a woods road. The path

enters the woods and is identified by red paint blazes. It rises steadily and becomes more of a mountain trail as it bears right into spruces. It climbs left again to a junction with the Green Trail. Above, through the spruces, you see the fire lookout's woodshed and cabin. The summit is directly beyond, surrounded by spruces; ledges support the steel tower.

Belknap Mountain is worthwhile climbing even on a hazy day. Although distant mountains are obscured, the nearer Lakes Region and Lake Winnipesaukee's varied shorelines appear in a

bird's-eye view. The lake is busy with boats. There is activity and traffic on roads in the Laconia-Weirs Beach area. For contrast, the woods stretch away east to the bare summit of Mount Major. A pond at the east base along NH 11A shows that beavers have taken over an old hay field. Belknap Mountain's blueberries resemble packaged varieties in supermarkets, but a handful will remind you what blueberries are supposed to taste like.

Return to the parking area easily by the service route, the Green Trail.

Belknap Mountain

Indian Pipe

Like Stinson Mountain to the northwest, Plymouth Mountain's high ridge is especially suitable in the spring as an introduction to a season of climbing. Or you may want to visit it in the fall when the foliage is most colorful and when snow has already chilled the more northern peaks.

Plymouth Mountain, although visible from Interstate 93 southwest of Plymouth, is little known and unspoiled. It is steep, yet undemanding. Because it rises in the Pemigewasset River valley and has a variety of trees and terrain, the slopes are alive in May with migrating birds. Sometimes the annual arrival of the warblers happens before the leaves unfold. Then you can spot the little birds clearly. The summit's evergreens and ledges attract juncos and white-throated sparrows. You see more birds than mountain views, although from one or two ledges you look north toward the Franconia Range and gain a perspective up the beautiful valley leading to Franconia Notch.

Among the many birds, the black-throated, blue warblers

Plymouth Mountain

12. Plymouth Mountain

Distance (round trip): 3 miles.
Walking time: 2 hours.
Vertical rise: 770 feet.

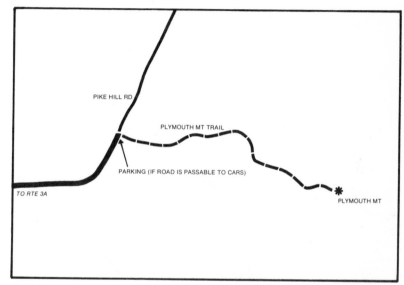

seem to favor Plymouth Mountain as late as the last ten days of May after the leaves are fully out. Watch for the slate-blue back of the male, with the identifying touch of white on the wings, and the black throat above a white breast. His notes are an odd buzzing series with a rising inflection at the end. Trace the sound high up in the oaks and beeches, and you may catch the singer in your binoculars.

During this latter part of May, there will be little green carpets of dwarf ginseng, the leaflets topped with frilly white blooms. The occasional large oaks, beeches, and yellow birches have an undergrowth of lesser trees sheltering other wild flowers and ferns. This forest changes to spruce and fir along the ridge in a manner typical of these New Hampshire elevations, here reaching 2,187 feet.

Follow NH 25 west from Plymouth. Turn south on NH 3A at the rotary, and drive toward Newfound Lake. Approaching the northern end of the lake, watch for the right turn to Hebron and Groton, but don't take it. Opposite this, left, is a dirt road known as Pike Hill Road. Don't attempt to drive it in the springtime or after heavy rain; instead, walk the country mile uphill to the start of the Plymouth Mountain Trail.

Watch for the trail on the right of Pike Hill Road, across from open fields and A-frames on the left. The trail starts opposite the remains of a brick house, now merely bricks in the bushes. At first, the trail is a woods road. It leads over a low knoll to a clearing, a beaver pond, and a small brook, then crosses the brook. It enters the woods and begins to climb beyond a log brow once used for rolling logs onto trucks. Markers for the trail are tin-can tops nailed to trees, and small board signs, each with a stenciled black wolf in one corner, put up by Camp Mowglis.

After a steady rise, the trail swings left, gets steeper, and comes out on a bare ledge, fine for picnics. Beyond this ledge, the trail leads down and up again through spruces, mostly along the ridge, to the cairn and tree-grown rocks of the summit.

Steep, wooded slopes and ledges hide this bare summit above Lake Winnipesaukee's Alton Bay. Mount Major surprises you with the extent of the outlook in all directions, but you are primarily attracted to the lake, for this is a lakeshore mountain.

The new scenic highway section of NH 11 runs above the west shore of Alton Bay. Five miles north from the summer resort of that name, a western ridge conceals Mount Major's flat crown. A highway sign identifies the parking area for hikers. This is ½ mile north of the parking for motorists' views across the lake. The Mount Major Trail starts from the northwest corner of the parking area, beyond the line of guard rocks, on the edge of the woods.

The graded path climbs through a little valley of oaks, maples, and hemlocks. Then steeper, it begins a swing west—here it is joined by a logging road from the right—and levels out. On this west side of the mountain, you leave the highway and the lake behind. Old stone walls strike off among the oaks. On the right

Stone Hut on Mt. Major

Mount Major

13. Mount Major

Distance (round trip): 2½ miles.
Walking time: 1¾ hours.
Vertical rise: 1,000 feet.

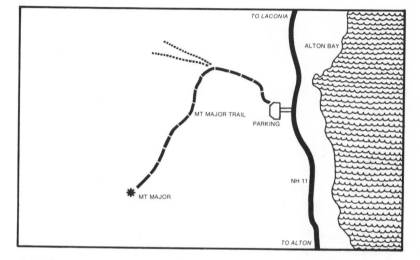

side, a cellar hole indicates the site of an ancient farmhouse. Now, the pileated woodpecker digs at the forest's dead stubs.

After ¼ mile, a branch road turns left at a trail sign on a tree. A short climb brings you to the mountain trail as the road bears right. There is little chance of error here because the logging roads are unused and the trail is plain.

Swinging left and winding over stones and among pines, the trail grows steeper and approaches the first ledges through a short, narrow trough worn in rotten rock. In early June, there are pink lady's slippers flowering. Columbine blossoms beside the rocks. At the ledges, look behind you for the first high views of Lake Winnipesaukee.

Low-bush blueberries grow along the trail. Wild cherries, pines, young white birch, and mountain maple extend into the blueberry patches. The trail reaches the final ledges. These are at first sharp and in places sheer for a few feet, putting you to handholds and careful footholds. This is scrambling, not rock climbing. The upper ledges are worn by glaciers and by

exposure, but the coarse, notched surfaces are readily surmounted. On the open summit, a four-sided stone shelter stands out against the sky. Roofless, its rock slabs are set in mortar. Various outlooks extend from the broad center ledges. The views sweep around you, but the lake catches and holds your attention.

Long and narrow, Alton Bay extends to the south. Northward the big lake stretches to the east shore and the town of Wolfeboro. Directly north is the length of Rattlesnake Island. Beyond, the blue water extends northwesterly broken by many islands and peninsulas, or "necks," which blend in the distance with

the reaches of the lake and the wooded slopes rising to the Ossipee Mountains. Often in summer, haze obscures the farther mountains. To the west, Belknap Mountain's tower marks that summit, above lesser, forested ridges.

Mount Major, open rock except for blueberry bushes and small birches, exposes you to cooling breezes, welcome after the climb.

Descend by the same route. After the level swing around from the west, remember to turn right, downhill, off the logging road and into the graded path above the parking area.

Alone and easily accessible from the Baker River valley, Stinson Mountain has the specialties and charms of smaller mountains. Its elevation of 2,870 feet treats the hiker to the joy of arriving at the summit after just enough effort and distance to impart a sense of accomplishment. This delight, compounded of well-being, good luck, and the wide view, has more to do with why people climb mountains than the commonly accepted motive "because it's there."

The fire tower provides the final vantage point above the rocks and evergreens. Forests, mountains, and lakes surround the lovely rural valley along Baker River with its farms and houses. The Franconia Range and the Sandwich Range are north and east. The village of Rumney lies at the foot of the mountain, Stinson Lake in the hollow to the north, Campton Bog to the east. Lesser-known mountains on the west—Mount Cube, Smarts Mountain, Piermont Mountain, Carr Mountain—are clothed in forests. To the

Trillium

Stinson Mountain

14. Stinson Mountain

Distance (round trip): 4 miles.
Walking time: 2¼ hours.
Vertical rise: 1,390 feet.

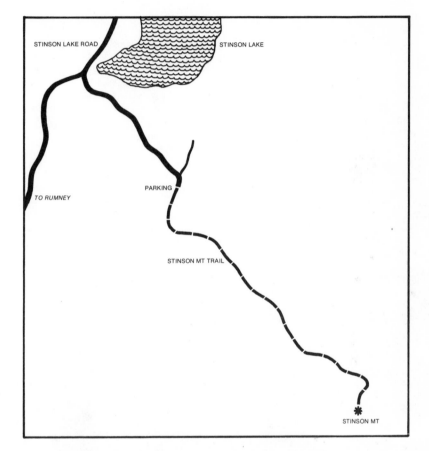

north, Mount Moosilauke rises above treeline.

Pleasant and varied in any season from spring to late fall, Stinson Mountain is especially fine in October, not only for the trail, which rises through leafed woods of red and yellow, but for the blends of colors spreading out in all directions from the summit. By then the cone of Mount Moosilauke is sometimes snowcapped.

Drive west from Plymouth on NH 25 to Rumney. Turn north through the village to Stinson Lake. Bear right near the outlet of the lake and continue uphill to a sharp left turn: Swing right a few yards and park opposite a field and house. This former town road continues as the trail after it fords a small brook running off the mountain, which is now visible to its summit and fire tower.

This old road continues straight for about ¼ mile, then the trail turns left through woods and along stone walls to an old cellar hole, which it passes on a left corner. Large trees grow in the old cellar. The trail ascends gradually to a trickling brook, which cannot be counted on for water in dry seasons. The trail here leads right, away from a plank bridge and logging road; it ascends, switching twice to steeper grades, and passes an opening at the telephone line, with a view over Stinson Lake and toward Mount Moosilauke. Entering spruce and fir woods interspersed with striped maple and mountain ash for the last climb, the trail curves right and breaks out all at once into the clearing by the warden's cabin and the rocks under the fire lookout tower.

Stinson Mountain

15. Mount Cardigan

Distance (around the loop): 3½ miles.
Walking time: 2½ hours.
Vertical rise: 1,220 feet.

A crown of solid rock forms the top of Mount Cardigan. As you approach the fire tower lookout exposed to the open sky and wind, you are taken by the illusion of climbing on the barren rock of some remote and mightier mountain; instead you are on an outpost of the White Mountains at only 3,121 feet elevation. The illusion is dispelled by the sight of initials and dates carved in the rock over the years. Cardigan has been a popular climb for a long time, and many trails ascend it.

The route of this hike is a loop from the Cardigan State Reservation's parking and picnic area, up the West Ridge Trail and a return via South Peak and the South Ridge Trail. Access roads approach through the towns west of the mountain, Canaan and Orange.

Cardigan's distinctive rock dome is extended by the lower ledges of the north and south ridges. The rock is known as Cardigan pluton. It is a form of Kinsman quartz monzonite common in New Hampshire and is part of a formation at various levels, sixty miles long and twelve miles wide extending from West Peterborough to north of Groton.

Here on Cardigan, forest fires destroyed the trees and organic earth, and erosion exposed the bare rock. In 1855, a fire twisted up in flame and smoke from the north ridge so spectacularly and with such destruction that the rock is still largely barren, and the ridge is named "Firescrew," from the spiraling smoke and flames that were visible in all the villages for miles around.

The south ridge is also open rock, with only scattered evergreens. Views from South Peak are mostly east and west. But pick a clear day. Summer haze, which spoils the view, can sometimes be avoided by making an early morning climb.

About the first week in May, the lower forested slopes of hardwoods show the greenery of new leaves while trees above are still bare or only budded. In the fall, the first yellow and red leaves appear near the summit, while the lower trees remain green. Changes requiring weeks at a single elevation appear in one glance down the mountainside.

Also, in spring and fall, watch out for ice on the rock. You could slide a long way into the trees with time to think about other errors before the crash.

Growing below the South Peak's ridge, in May, will be dogtooth violets—really members of the lily family—and small yellow violets, purple trillium, and wood anemone. In summer, look for the flat leaves of the green-flowered orchis.

Binoculars are useful to study the lakes and farther ranges, or to peer into towns, or to watch a raven near the summit. This bird from the north has been seen recently on Cardigan. Warblers flock to the wooded slopes at migration time.

During the heavy winds that sweep across the rock, a climb to the tower, by invitation of the lookout, will give you an unbelievable "ride." The glassed-in room seems to rush downwind in a rocking, roaring rumble, straining against the cables. In a high wind, the tower sounds and feels like a subway car.

On Mt. Cardigan

Mount Cardigan

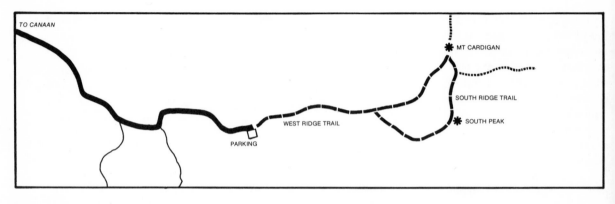

The view, starting west and looking counterclockwise, extends to Vermont, then Massachusetts, then east over the New Hampshire Lakes Region and the Belknaps, and around to the northeast, where the Sandwich Range is moored by the pinnacle of Mount Chocorua. Perhaps clouds swirl over the distant Presidentials and Franconias. Mount Moosilauke, northward, may be impressively white in early spring and late fall.
To the northwest where four townships meet by Bryant Pond, a ridge running south is scarred by old mica mines.

To reach the west side of the mountain and the West Ridge Trail, drive to Canaan on US 4. Turn north on NH 118, and soon take a right on the road to

Orange. Beyond the town hall and school, which are on the left, continue straight, over the bridge spanning Orange Brook. The road forks. Keep right, on the Grafton Road, for about ¾ mile to another fork. Turn left up to the entrance to Cardigan State Park and the ½ mile of road leading to the parking area and picnic tables.

The West Ridge Trail leaves the picnic clearing at a sign on the edge of the woods and climbs by easy stages, passing two springs in the first ¾ mile. Keep left past the South Ridge Trail, which offers the best views as part of the return loop. Above this junction, a short, side climb leads to outlooks to the right and then rejoins the main West Ridge Trail. Walk past the Skyland Trail, which is

a ridge route to Alexandria Four Corners.

The West Ridge Trail crosses a footbridge, leads past an open-front shelter, passes two branch trails, and ascends steeply over rock, along a route identified by cairns and white paint, to the lookout tower.

In descending, go down to the lookout's cabin, bear right from the junction with the Clark Trail, and take the South Ridge Trail. This leads you over partially wooded ledges beyond South Peak, with its great views, to Rimrock, then crosses Skyland Trail, and slabs around through woods to the West Ridge Trail at the junction you passed on the way up, about ¾ mile above the parking area.

Mount Cardigan

Franconia Notch Region

View from Artist Bluff

Franconia Notch with its state park and famous Profile, two lakes, the Tramway, and ski trails, all bordering US 3, has too many attractions for a quick visit. Don't try to see all the lakes, streams, precipices, and rock formations in a day. Along with Cannon Mountain, Eagle Cliff, and Mount Lafayette, they are overpowering. First, get a hiker's perspective. If time is short and the urge to escape speeding cars and wandering tourists is imperative, climb Artist Bluff and Bald Mountain at the north end of the Notch. You need only an hour or two. But don't procrastinate. It may be your last chance to see the relatively unspoiled Notch before the highway-program juggernaut blasts Interstate 93 through this historic and scenic mountain pass.

Stop and look at the Profile— New Hampshire's unique "Old Man of the Mountains." Then drive north on US 3 past the Tramway and its cable cars up Cannon Mountain. Keep Echo Lake on your left. At the end of the lake turn left onto NH 18, which soon brings you to the parking area for Echo Lake Beach. Leave your car there.

Artist Bluff and Bald Mountain

16. Artist Bluff and Bald Mountain

Distance (round trip): 1½ miles.
Walking time: 1¼ hours.
Vertical rise: 400 feet.

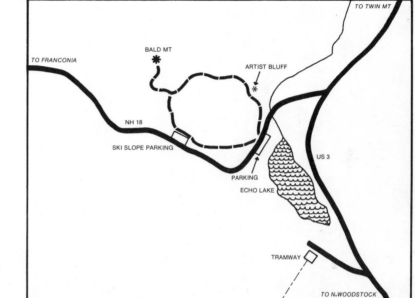

The trail to Artist Bluff starts on the north side of NH 18. Walk back east from the parking area. The trail is on your left near a highway route sign and west of the outlet from Echo Lake. Climb the highway embankment by a path worn in the gravel. It enters the woods and leads up among big rocks. There's a steep climb up a gully.

Near the top, you turn right on a spur trail a few yards to Artist Bluff. This is a rock cliff from which artists might paint the Notch, but it's more often a vantage point for photographers. The view is magnificent across Echo Lake to Eagle Cliff and Mount Lafayette, left, and to Cannon Mountain on the right.

For a complete hike above the north and western gateways of the Notch, return to the trail and turn right. Climb the remainder of the gully and over the wooded height above. The trail leads up and down over the knolls. You pass another ledge lookoff before you descend to the sag below Bald Mountain's summit. Watch for the tall old spruces along the trail. Most of them have been struck by lightning, and their trunks bear

the vertical scars. The trail joins a former carriage road up from NH 18. Turn right for Bald Mountain. Climb the trail by a series of steps over rock from the first switchback.

On the rocky open summit you stand clear of the small spruces. You look west over Franconia village, far away to the Connecticut River valley, and into Vermont. Cannon Mountain's ski slopes are south. Turning around left, you look into the deep Notch, again across Echo Lake.

Return to the junction with the Artist Bluff Trail. Turn right and follow the trail down the graded, ancient carriage road to NH 18. It ends at the parking area for skiers on the Roland Peabody Memorial Slope. Keep left along the bank above the parking area. An unmarked trail leads through the woods back to the Echo Lake Beach parking area. Or you may walk back along NH 18.

Mount Pemigewasset

17. Mount Pemigewasset

Distance (round trip): 2½ miles.
Walking time: 2 hours.
Vertical rise: 1,150 feet.

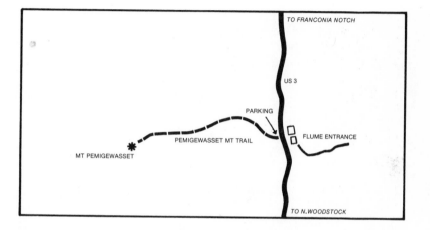

Mount Pemigewasset, at the south end of Franconia Notch, is the buttress for the Indian Head, whose impassive profile looks down upon the motels and restaurants along US 3 north of North Woodstock. It is also a summit with extensive views. The mountain extends north from the cliffs forming the Indian Head, and the trail to the summit from that direction starts opposite the entrance to the Flume. The open ledges at the end of the climb give the mountain an individuality that is more spectacular than its height would suggest, for its elevation is only 2,554 feet, less than half that of Mount Lafayette five miles away to the northeast.

After the tourist attractions of the Notch, you'll be refreshed by this climb above the highway and by the view of the mountains or down the valley. At sunset, you watch the horizon glow, and you are treated to a much rarer sight: the low-angled shadows and the brilliancy of late sun on the peaks of the Notch, a series of gleaming crests above the purple valley.

On the Pemigewasset Mountain Trail

It will be time then to return the 1¼ miles to the highway and your car. For a sunset hike, take a flashlight with new batteries, and a picnic supper in a small knapsack. If you linger on the mountain, you will find that the twilight of the summit has changed to darkness down by US 3.

In the days of mountain inns, instead of returning to a parked car, you would have crossed a lawn to the lights and hospitality of the Flume House.

To reach the trail, park on the west side of US 3, across from the Flume buildings. The Pemigewasset Mountain Trail starts at the south end of this parking area. It crosses a small open

picnic space, and, at the upper left, enters the woods as an improved path. After ½ mile, this path joins a much older trail and swings left, upward along that route, then above a small brook, which the trail meets but does not cross. It turns sharply right up a bank. A steady climb takes you to the north side of the mountain and the beginning of spruce and fir growing among the hardwoods. Entering from the right is a trail sometimes used to circle the base of the cliffs from the Indian Head Cabins on US 3. The Pemigewasset Mountain Trail leads on to the broad ledges above the cliffs at the summit.

Mount Pemigewasset

Georgiana Falls

18. Georgiana Falls

Distance (round trip): 2½ miles.
Walking time: 1½ hours.
Vertical rise: 700 feet.

Harvard Brook, a western tributary of the Pemigewasset River above North Woodstock, drops over ledges on a steep ridge. After rains or in early summer when brooks are full, Georgiana Falls gush as shining cascades down into a pool.
In his classic *The White Hills* (Boston, 2d ed., 1887, pp. 125–26; 1st ed., 1859), Thomas Starr King describes the approach to the falls as a "splendid line of light through the trees and shrubbery that fringe the rocky cleft," and declares them to be "one of the grandest cascades of the mountain region."

The water dwindles in late summer, and the spectacular flow requires a rainstorm to renew itself. There are two sets of falls. The upper one, ½ mile above Georgiana Falls, is known as Harvard Falls. The discovery is attributed to some exploring Harvard students before 1858, but, as the state of New Hampshire built the highway through the Notch—a muddy, stony, rough track—about 1813, curious travelers very likely arrived at the cascades earlier. Or fishermen, lured farther and farther up-

Georgiana Falls, late summer.

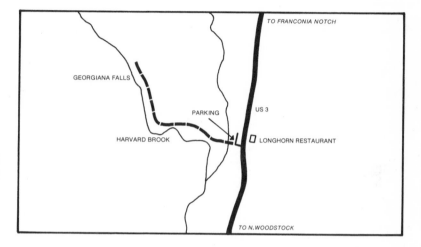

stream, may have caught trout in the pools below the falls.
At present, the cascades appear from US 3 during May and June as a distant, strange, white patch on the greenery, like lingering snow.

The trail once maintained by the Forest Service has been abandoned, but hikers have kept open a path from a logging road to the falls. If, or when, Interstate 93 goes through, access will have to be changed.

Drive north from North Woodstock on US 3 past the bordering motels, restaurants, ice cream stands, and gift shops. You may wonder whether there's a hike into the deep woods any-

where near. But continue about 2¼ miles from North Woodstock. Approaching the Longhorn Restaurant on the right, turn left (west) off the highway on a side road. Keep to the road for 200 feet. At a right turn, drive straight into a parking place at Hanson Brook. Cross the brook on foot to a logging road. This leads to Harvard Brook. Turn right, upstream; don't cross Harvard Brook. Follow a logging road up the east bank past various branch roads for ½ mile, where the road becomes a trail. It leads along and up Harvard Brook to the final climb to the pool and the falls. The rocks are slippery when wet, but the air is cool and moist.

Georgiana Falls

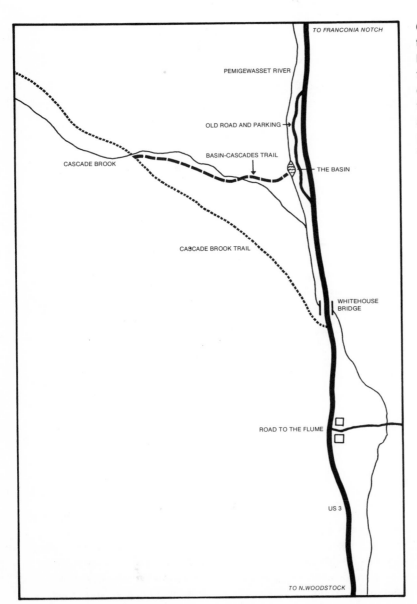

TO FRANCONIA NOTCH

PEMIGEWASSET RIVER

OLD ROAD AND PARKING →

BASIN-CASCADES TRAIL

CASCADE BROOK

— THE BASIN

CASCADE BROOK TRAIL

WHITEHOUSE
BRIDGE

ROAD TO THE FLUME

US 3

TO N. WOODSTOCK

Basin-Cascades Trail

Of the various trails maintained in the Notch by the New Hampshire Division of Parks, the Basin-Cascades Trail is one of the most interesting. It passes through woods of fine stature and it climbs up beside falls, pool, and rock formations along the way.

The Basin-Cascades Trail may be considered a link from the Basin to Cascade Brook Trail, which leads on to Lonesome Lake, but for hikers exploring the Notch it is an experience in itself for an afternoon in mountain woods.

North of the Flume about 1½ miles, the old road through the Notch has been preserved to the west of US 3 and gives access to the big glacial pothole called the Basin. There are parking places and picnic tables.

To reach the Basin-Cascades Trail, cross the lower footbridge at the Basin and follow a path that branches right into the woods. This will soon be joined by the Pemi-Trail coming down from Lafayette Campground. (The Pemi-Trail and the Profile Lake Trail north of Lafayette Campground make it possible to walk about 4 miles

19. Basin-Cascades Trail

Distance (to Cascade Brook Trail and back): 3 miles.
Walking time: 2 hours.
Vertical rise: 500 feet.

The Basin

Much of this trip is through woods that should remind hikers to be thankful for the successful efforts of the Society for the Protection of New Hampshire Forests, which saved the Notch from loggers.

An old-timer, who was a child in the 1920s, may remember giving a dollar—assisted by his parents perhaps—for a tree, in the Society's campaign, "Buy a Tree to Help Save the Notch." Major contributions came from philanthropists interested in conservation. Women's clubs, newspapers, and the Appalachian Mountain Club also contributed, as did the New Hampshire taxpayers through their legislature, which appropriated half the $400,000 required to buy the 6,000 acres along seven miles of US 3. Dedication ceremonies were held on September 15, 1928, at Profile Lake below the "Old Man of the Mountains." Dedication was to the New Hampshire men and women who had served the nation in time of war.

But the Notch needs saving again: this time from the dynamite and bulldozers of highway promoters who can spoil it as the loggers with axe and saw almost did forty-five years ago.

along the Pemigewasset River, with easy grades and footbridges, between the Basin and Profile Lake.)

At the junction with the Pemi-Trail, the Basin-Cascades Trail bears left toward Cascade Brook. It follows the north bank past cascades and past Kinsman Falls. Above the falls, the trail crosses the brook, leads up a steep bank, and continues to follow the brook through woods, past more falls, and between two interesting rock dikes. It leads, gradually climbing, to the junction with the Cascade Brook Trail. The Cascade Brook Trail, between Lonesome Lake and US 3 at Whitehouse Bridge, is a link in the Appalachian Trail from Maine to Georgia.

Hikers with the time, energy, and eagerness to visit Lonesome Lake may follow Cascade Brook Trail to the right 1½ miles farther to the lake and the AMC Hut there. Those who aren't quite up to this 6-mile round trip from the Basin can turn back and enjoy the descent along the same Basin-Cascades Trail, saving an excursion to Lonesome Lake for another day.

Lonesome Lake

20. Lonesome Lake

Distance (round trip): 3¼ miles.
Walking time: 2¾ hours.
Vertical rise: 1,000 feet.

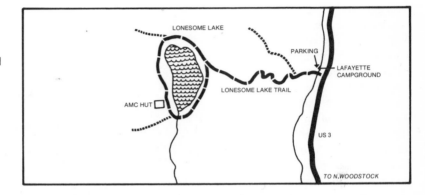

One thousand feet above Franconia Notch is Lonesome Lake, a goal for climbers and visitors who take advantage of the graded trail to walk in and see a true mountain lake in a spectacular setting. No longer "lonesome," quite the opposite, the much-used trails, along with the plywood hut of the AMC, and the voices of hikers with their colorful packs and clothes, give a modern touch to the ancient scenery.

The lake has been popular since the days of mountain inns after the Civil War. The trail still follows the old bridle path, along which many vacationers from the now-vanished hotels rode to the lake for the magnificent views of the mountains on both sides of the Notch.

Legend names President Ulysses S. Grant as one of the notable visitors. According to the story, he came to the Notch and the Profile House in 1869. A yellow coach and six bay horses driven by Ed Cox, a famous "whip," brought him from Bethlehem in fifty-five minutes—a fantastic rate of more than thirteen

Lonesome Lake

miles an hour. In later years, a steam train and rails brought guests to the Profile House, which burned in August 1923.

The views from Lonesome Lake are, indeed, great—comprehensive, craggy, wild, and dominated by the treeless peak of Mount Lafayette. From the lake, trails lead to Cannon Mountain, Mount Kinsman, and Kinsman Pond. The Appalachian Trail passes by the lower end of the lake.

As many as forty-six hikers can be accommodated at the AMC's Lonesome Lake Hut, situated on the west shore facing the Franconia Range. There is a trail around the lake, ¾ mile, passing the site of old log cabins. A stand of tamarack makes a fine display of yellow in the fall. The lake is 2,734 feet above

sea level. Westward, the ever-green forest rises to the ledges of Mount Kinsman.

Park at Lafayette Place. This is a clearing, picnic area, and campground between the Profile and the Flume on the west side of US 3. When you leave your car, pause and walk around until you can see the best view of the cliffs of Cannon Mountain.

The Lonesome Lake Trail will be found by walking beyond the picnic area. Near the south end is a stream that's already called by its full name, Pemigewasset River. Cross this on the footbridge. Walk through the campground following yellow trail blazes to the entrance into the woods. Very shortly, the trail begins the series of graded switchbacks up the steep slope.

You surmount most of the 1,000 feet to the lake in the ridge's first ½ mile. You work your way upward by the switchbacks originally designed for horses and riders, but now equally useful to hikers. Pass by the Hi-Cannon Trail on the right. The Lonesome Lake Trail continues to climb. The ridge, which looked so easy from Lafayette Place, seems to have deceived you. But the trail soon begins to level out, and, after about 1 mile, you detect a slight descent. The lake is ahead in its flat wooded setting. You come to a trail junction.

To reach the AMC Hut, take the **Cascade Brook Trail**, which branches left from the Lonesome Lake Trail. Follow along the east shore of the lake until you come to another trail junction at the lake's south end. Turn right on the Fishin' Jimmy Trail across the outlet, and take the left fork to the AMC Hut.

For the return route, walk the Around-Lonesome-Lake Trail on the west shore to a junction with the Lonesome Lake Trail north of the lake. Turn right. Keep past the Cascade Brook Trail, and you are on the way back down to Lafayette Place.

Lonesome Lake

21. Mount Flume

Distance (round trip via Flume Slide Trail): 8 miles.
(round trip via Mount Liberty loop): 8¼ miles.
Walking time (either way): 6½ hours.
Vertical rise (Flume Slide Trail only): 2,927 feet.
(including Mount Liberty loop): 3,327 feet.

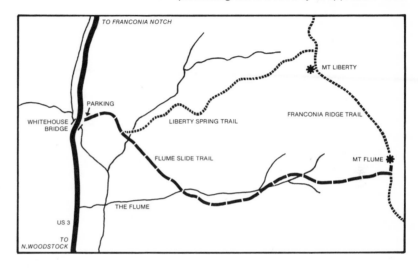

Appearing as a rocky pinnacle to the drivers and passengers northbound on Interstate 93 and US 3 into Woodstock, Mount Flume sets the style for the Franconia Range. This southern terminus of the long ridge above treeline is a fitting introduction to Mount Liberty, Mount Lincoln, and Mount Lafayette. But Mount Flume has its own distinction, namely, the slide, which you climb via the Flume Slide Trail.

Mount Flume overlooks the rock chasm and cascades near US 3 and the entrance to Franconia Notch, known to generations of sightseers as the Flume. Formerly, the Flume served hikers as an access route to trails up both Mount Flume and its northern neighbor, Mount Liberty. Trail relocation in 1972 moved the starting point for these climbs north to the Appalachian Trail crossing on US 3.

To reach the Flume Slide Trail, drive north from North Woodstock on US 3 past the Flume entrance. Proceed ¾ mile to Whitehouse Bridge spanning the young Pemigewasset River. A

Climbers on Franconia Ridge

sign identifies the Appalachian Trail where it comes out of the woods, left. Drive across the bridge. Turn right for parking, picnic tables, and trail signs.

Walking east across the parking area, you come to the beginning of the Liberty Spring Trail, which takes you up fairly steeply through the hardwoods ¾ mile to the Flume Slide Trail. Bear right at this fork. (The Liberty Spring Trail continues toward Liberty Spring Campsite and Mount Liberty.)

The Flume Slide Trail leads to the former route above the Flume. There, you begin the easterly climb up the first of a

series of old logging roads leading to the base of the slide.

The last water is a brook before you reach the slide. The upper ridge is dry. It is also dangerous when closed in by clouds and rain, particularly during summer thunder storms; then there is plenty of water in the form of rain, but a lightning bolt might end your climbing.

The challenge of Mount Flume begins at the slide. For more than ½ mile, you face the side of the mountain where once an avalanche of rocks and gravel poured down. Now somewhat grown to small birches and evergreens, it still keeps your

Mount Flume

eyes focused on footholds and handholds. Pause for the views opening across the Notch to Mount Kinsman and Cannon Mountain. Climbing here for those with packs is easier than descending—except for the demand on lungs—but caution is required either way. Double your care if rain has soaked the rocks.

At the top of the slide keep left as the trail enters spruces and firs, climbing to the junction with the Franconia Ridge Trail. At the right, the Osseo Trail leads south over wooded Osseo Peak to the Kancamagus Highway almost 6 miles away.

Follow the Franconia Ridge Trail left up into the spruce scrub to the edge of the open cliffs above the slide you have climbed. A few yards to the north is the summit of the peak, a small area of rock. The effect is immediate—a sense of achievement and emergence from a hard climb to an extreme height. Elevation, 4,327 feet. The view is grand in all directions.

Northward, you see the barren and rocky crests of Mount Liberty, Mount Lincoln, and Mount Lafayette, highest in the range. Turning west, you look across the Notch to the humped summits of Mount Kinsman, and, at the head of the Notch, Cannon Mountain bulking above the Profile's cliffs, which show no indication of the silhouette. To the east, your eyes sweep over the forested valleys draining into the Pemigewasset River's East Branch. The far ridge in this Pemigewasset "Wilderness" rises north from cliffs to Mount Bond's treeless summit. Mount Carrigain, farther east, bounds the "Wilderness" with its massive pyramid topped by a fire tower.

If the afternoon is only beginning and the weather remains fine, you can yield to the appeal of another summit, Mount Liberty, down and up 1¼ miles north along the Franconia Ridge Trail. Beyond the peak, turn left down the Liberty Spring Trail for completion of a loop back to your car.

But Mount Liberty is a good climb by itself. Save it for another day unless your vacation is running out. Return down the Flume Slide Trail, as you climbed, and watch your footing on the slide.

Mount Flume

22. Mount Liberty

Distance (round trip): 6 miles.
Walking time: 5 hours.
Vertical rise: 3,060 feet.

The ledgy crest of Mount Liberty lines up with the higher Franconia Range northward and provides closer views of the Notch from a better angle than Mount Flume. Instead of a slide for a final approach, the Liberty Spring Trail leads up past a campsite popular with Appalachian Trail hikers.

Mt. Liberty

The climb, like the one up Mount Flume (see hike number 21), begins at Whitehouse Bridge. Drive ¾ mile up US 3 past the Flume entrance. The highway tops a hill and dips down to the bridge and to the parking area on the right, where you'll find trail signs and picnic tables.

The Liberty Spring Trail runs east out of the parking area.

Climb ¾ mile to the fork where Flume Slide Trail branches right. Keep left, as the Liberty Spring Trail continues up through the hardwood forest, crosses a brook, and climbs to join a former route from the Flume.

Steadily rising, the trail takes you up slopes once logged and burned. In 1917, hikers, climbing among rocks scorched bare by

Mount Liberty

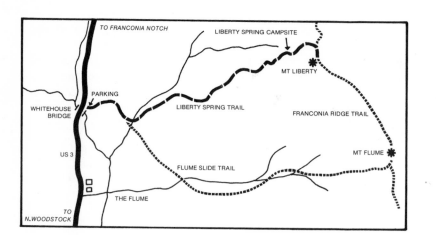

a forest fire, followed signs nailed to blackened stubs.

The trail swings up steeply to your right, then becomes more gradual, and passes Liberty Spring Campsite. (No shelter here; tent platforms only. Last water.) On up through the spruce/fir woods you climb to the Franconia Ridge Trail. Turn right (south) and follow the Franconia Ridge Trail up into the open, where you see the steep rocky summit ahead. You feel that lift of excitement from the expanse of sky and mountain, and from the certainty that you'll soon surmount the last rocks.

This 4,460-foot peak overlooks the great forests to the east in the Pemigewasset "Wilderness."

Northward, along the Franconia Ridge Trail, your gaze adjusts to the increasing height beyond Little Haystack Mountain, where narrow ledges rise to Mount Lincoln. On the left a distant green ridge curves down from AMC's Greenleaf Hut into the Notch below Mount Lafayette, which Mount Lincoln obscures. North, across the Notch, the high cliffs of Cannon Mountain appear chopped from the wooded summit. Westward, Mount Kinsman's slope and long, summit ridge parallel the highway. In the opposite direction, east, Owl's Head, more like a great whale, fills the valley north toward Mount Garfield. Over Owl's Head, past Mount Guyot, the peak on the northeastern

horizon is Mount Washington. And all around, distant under a clear sky and high clouds, the mountains seem endless.

Often, however, Mount Liberty is in cloud, and the wind is cold. But luck favors the prepared hiker; if you carry, in a pack, plenty of extra clothing and rain parka, maybe you won't need them; then you can sit in the sun and enjoy your sandwiches and Liberty Spring water from your canteen.

The descent takes you north along the Franconia Ridge Trail on the same route you climbed. Turn left onto the Liberty Spring Trail, which you follow back to your car.

Mount Liberty

23. Mount Lincoln

Distance (round trip, Mount Lincoln only): 7 miles.
(around the loop, Lincoln and Lafayette): 8 miles.
Walking time (Mount Lincoln only): 5¾ hours.
(around the loop): 7½ hours.
Vertical rise (to Mount Lincoln): 3, 350 feet.
(around the loop): 3,750 feet.*

To many hikers along the Franconia Ridge Trail, Mount Lincoln is a way station on the high line of peaks knifing north and south above Franconia Notch east of US 3. But Mount Lincoln can be a fine destination in itself. During the ascent, you will see spectacular waterfalls, a unique slanting cliff, alpine-arctic environment above treeline, and wide, wide views, especially overlooking the Pemigewasset "Wilderness" clear away to Crawford Notch and Mount Washington. This hike offers the added bonus of a climb up the highest peak in the Franconia Range, Mount Lafayette, if you wish.

Leave your car at Lafayette Place two miles south of the Tramway on the west side of US 3, where the state of New Hampshire maintains a picnic area and campground. Cross the highway. Pass through a gate and keep right, between

*Mount Lafayette is only 141 feet higher than Mount Lincoln, but the climb from the col north of Mount Lincoln is 400 feet.

state park buildings, to the Falling Waters Trail.

In the first ½ mile, you cross Walker Brook flowing from a ravine on Mount Lafayette, and you ascend gradually, swinging through woods of maple, beech, and yellow birch, for another ½ mile to Dry Brook. Contrary to its name, the brook is a crystal torrent in early summer.

You cross Dry Brook to the south Bank and begin a steeper climb. You pass cascades on the left and approach ledges high up in the trees. The trail appears to end at a pool in a narrow ravine. Swiftwater Falls gush into the pool from a ledge sixty feet high. You see the trail to the left of the falls. You cross to the opposite bank over rocks at the foot of the pool.

The climb begins here in earnest, although the trail is graded, and sections of it follow old logging roads. You were impressed by Swiftwater Falls. Now Cloudland Falls, twenty feet higher, descends toward you in a white, shifting curtain sliding into the gorge.

Above Cloudland Falls, from the steep and slippery ledge, you first look out across the valley. Keep to the north bank. The trail continues up rough and steep as the brook branches into the upper growth of spruce and fir. You climb a section of weathered rock debris. You look up at a smooth granite face looming across the mountainside and gleaming in the sun when wet, which it usually is because of drainage from its brow of trees. This is Shining Rock Cliff.

The trail climbs up left along the base of the cliff. In the next ½ mile it clears the scrub of treeline in a steep ascent into the open rockery of Little Haystack, a minor peak on the Franconia Ridge Trail.

If the wind blows rain, and clouds are settling into a blinding fog, this is a good place to turn back. Wait for a better day. The exciting panorama from the ridge demands a clear view. There's no value in a memory of Mount Lincoln as gray rocks packed in cotton batting. Besides, the ridge is

Mount Lincoln

dangerous in stormy weather. Lightning strikes frequently. Winds can be icy even in summer. You will be almost a mile up in the sky. The col between Little Haystack and Mount Lincoln is exposed, narrow, and in places almost sheer on each side.

In fine weather, turn north along the Franconia Ridge Trail and enjoy the ¾ mile above trees in the open exposure of sun and sky. The summit of Mount Lincoln is at 5,108 feet.

Multiplicities of mountains rise in all directions, and on the east the rocks fall away to green forests along Lincoln Brook and Franconia Branch, which flow around 4,023-foot Owl's Head anchored like a humped barge in the green sea of trees.

For a loop and return to your car, the Franconia Ridge Trail provides a clear-day bonus beyond Mount Lincoln. North, beyond Mount Lincoln's summit, the trail descends, down, over, and among rocks, all in the open, then up to Mount Lafayette's rugged slopes and summit cairn—a 1-mile hike

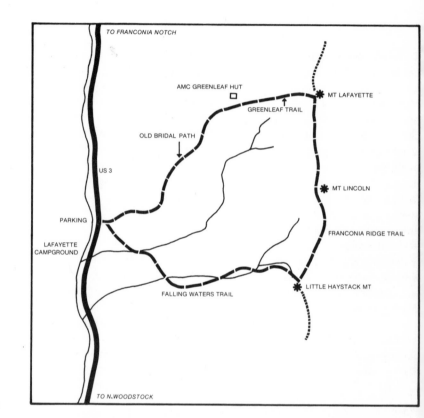

among alpine-arctic plants, such as diapensia, hugging the windswept ledges. From Mount Lafayette turn left and go down by the Greenleaf Trail to the AMC's Greenleaf Hut. Then take the Old Bridle Path for the descent along a ridge where, in June, the rhodora blossoms are showy pink above Walker Ravine. The Old Bridle Path

takes you to your starting point opposite Lafayette Place. If you don't choose to include the loop to Mount Lafayette, you may return from Mount Lincoln as you climbed and enjoy once again Shining Rock Cliff, Cloudland Falls, and Swiftwater Falls.

Mt. Lincoln

24. Mount Lafayette

Distance (round trip): 7 miles.
Walking time: 6 hours.
Vertical rise: 3,475 feet.

The "top of the world" in the Franconia Range is, of course, named for the French hero of the American Revolution. His 1825 visit to New Hampshire brought about the change from the peak's older name of Great Haystack. Its northwestern cliffs and slides form the east side of Franconia Notch above Profile Lake. Its long, forested slopes of beech and yellow birch rise above US 3 for two miles southward. Far up among the spruce scrub and barren rocks of treeline are two small lakes and the Greenleaf Hut of the AMC. The dwarf trees and ledges extend to a rock-strewn slope, 1 mile long, leading up to the summit, with rare mosses, plants, lichens, and grasses along the way.

The exposed stones of the peak could be arctic rather than in the temperate zone. Even on a summer day the wind often blows bitter cold. Plants are balanced on a delicate ecological margin. The dwarf spruces lie down before the wind and seem to grasp the rocks. Although doused with rain and

View of Mt. Lafayette

fog, the mountain cranberry and similar creeping plants are thick-leaved against dehydration from the wind. The leaves of the low shrub, Labrador tea, curl along the edges and are woolly underneath, thereby retarding evaporation of vital leaf moisture in the harsh winds. These mountain vines, prostrate bushes, and shrubby heaths blossom white, pink, and purple in early summer.

Mount Lafayette has long been a popular climb. The oldest trail, still called the Old Bridle Path, was more than a name once. Travelers rode up it on mountain ponies from the Lafayette House, which burned in 1861. Only foundation stones remain of the vanished summit house too, which in those days accommodated the successful climbers. When the AMC built Greenleaf Hut, burros bore loads up the path, and each year continued to transport supplies early in the season. Then, before the days of helicopters, the regular summer packing of necessary food and fuel depended on the legs and lungs of the hutmen lugging the long packboards. Still today, you will see hutmen treading

upwards under heavy loads.

The Old Bridle Path, leaving US 3 from the east side at Lafayette Place, is the scenic route up Lafayette. The views of the upper ridge and of Walker Ravine open out from a partially wooded shoulder halfway up to Greenleaf Hut. Starting as it does at the same point as the Falling Waters Trail, described in the Mount Lincoln climb, the Old Bridle Path forms a pleasant and easy link in that loop. (See hike number 23.)

A northerly and more challenging route from Franconia Notch up Mount Lafayette, the Greenleaf Trail, mounts beside Eagle Cliff and reaches the north slope through Eagle Pass, 1,000 feet above the Notch, and opposite the Profile.

Park at the area east of US 3, 10 miles north of North Woodstock, used by tourists who stop to view the profile of the Old Man. Walk north to the bank above the highway and beyond the parking area. A few cars are usually parked there where the Greenleaf Trail begins.

Don't let the graded path, the footbridge crossing between

Mount Lafayette

two ponds, nor the nature trail stations deceive you into thinking this is not a rugged mountain trail. The Greenleaf Trail parallels US 3 through open woods, and then strikes up the steep slope by a series of switchbacks. The footing is excellent and continues so on the upper trail as it curves north into Eagle Pass. You enter the pass under a long cliff similar to those towering still higher above. You pick your way over massive rocks as large as cottages, which have lodged in the pass. Snow and ice linger late in the gloomy caves below the boulders. If you leave the trail to explore, watch out for the treacherous patches of moss over the crevices. The trail itself is safe enough.

Beyond the rocky confines of Eagle Pass, the trail turns sharply right, south, on a side-hill slope and attacks the bulk of Mount Lafayette's north shoulder. The trail is steep and noted for its treacherous footing on loose stones. The trail rises at a lesser angle as it approaches the little reservoir for Greenleaf Hut and leads out of the evergreen

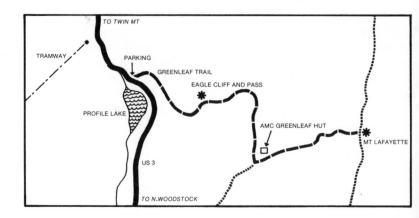

scrub to the open views and challenging barrens above treeline. The glacial age is long gone, but the ice scoured the rocks before it melted away leaving the great shards scattered precariously, a random and extravagant use of paving stones for men to wonder at.

Near the Hut, the Old Bridle Path joins the Greenleaf Trail. You descend beyond the Hut to the dwarf spruces again, then pass through the moist section at the little bog draining from the two basins of the Eagle Lakes. You climb above treeline once more and follow the worn pathway over the rocks. Massive cairns mark the route, which swings north for the final ascent.

If there's a storm brewing, turn around and leave the mountain to the lightning and thunder. (In 1970, two young men camping overnight at the summit were almost killed by lightning.) If there's a clear hour ahead, watch the high clouds and their shadows moving across the mountains. Don't try to count the peaks. There are too many. Look east at the miles of green trees, and remember that, before the days of the National Forest, the valleys were a blackened devastation of logged and burned ridges.

Return by the same route, the Greenleaf Trail, turning right, north, at the Hut for the descent to Eagle Pass.

Mount Lafayette

25. Cannon Mountain

Distance (round trip): 7¼ miles.
Walking time: 5½ hours.
Vertical rise: 2,100 feet.

You can ride in a Tramway cable car to the summit, so why climb Cannon Mountain on foot? Because only your two legs can make the mountain yours. Somehow this also improves the magnificent views of Franconia Notch and Mount Lafayette. For hikers aiming to climb all 4,000-footers, Cannon qualifies by 77 feet.

Skiers who have swooped down the snowy trails find that a summer climb, which pits them against this solid height unaided by Tramway or T-bars, gives the mountain new meaning.

A rounded block seen from the Notch, Cannon's stark cliffs loom before you as you drive north on US 3 toward the famous Profile. The mountain appears as a mass of stone on which evergreens cling with minimum success. Approach from the north, and you see its grassy ski slopes and trails like high pastures and giant paths down through the woods.

For a loop over the summit, climb the Kinsman Ridge Trail from the north and descend by the Hi-Cannon and Lonesome Lake Trails, returning through the Notch to your car via the Profile Lake Trail.

The Kinsman Ridge Trail begins its zig-zag climb about ¼ mile south of the Tramway. Watch for an asphalt roadway just south of the parking area west of US 3. Drive a few yards along this side road. Turn left onto a gravel track across a small field. Park at the edge of the woods.

This field, known as Profile Clearing, was the site of an immense old mountain hotel, the Profile House, which burned in 1923. From the field there's a view of the "cannon" that gave the mountain its name. If you walk to the field's center, turn around, and look west up the ridge in front of your car, you'll see a horizontal rock—the Cannon—outlined against the sky.

The Kinsman Ridge Trail climbs a bushy bank at the edge of the field a few yards south of a log cabin. At once you are on your way skyward. Steep for more than 1 mile, the trail gains altitude rapidly by a series of switchbacks. You hear the roar of the Tramway motors to the north. You climb to an opening in the trees and watch the cable cars slide gently up or down the black lines that suspend them.

The trail levels out on the east shoulder. After a passage through small spruce and fir, you come to a sharp right turn. A branch trail, unmarked, bears left to a breathtaking view from open ledges. North and south the Franconia crests line the horizon: Eagle Cliff, Mount Lafayette, Mount Lincoln, Little Haystack, and Mount Liberty.

On a ridge several hundred yards north, and from a camouflage of evergreen scrub, the Cannon aims at Mount Lafayette. From this angle it appears in its true form—a balanced rock shelf. You may wonder whether you're on the Profile's ledges. You're not. The Profile is dangerous, and reinforced rocks form the brooding silhouette far down and out of sight beyond the scrub and rocks.

Return to the main Kinsman Ridge Trail. Keep past the right turn leading back the way you came. The trail crosses

you see the Franconia Range, now part of a 360-degree view. Northward stretches the pastoral valley of the Gale River and Franconia village. South and west, a wilder panorama opens across Mount Kinsman's two summits toward Mount Moosilauke.

When you're ready to descend, return to the Kinsman Ridge Trail. Follow it where it passes southward below the summit from the junction where you turned up to the tower. (The trail continues its rugged way 15 miles to its southern end at the Lost River Road in Kinsman Notch.) Follow it only about ½ mile to the Hi-Cannon Trail where you turn left for the descent.

The Hi-Cannon Trail takes you past a lookoff ledge opening toward Mount Kinsman on your right and Lonesome Lake below you. The trail swings through young firs above cliffs from which there are wide outlooks into the Notch with its parallel ranges east and west. You climb down rocks on two short ladders and pass the eave-like ledges called Cliff House on your left.

Cannon Mountain

the east shoulder, then dips into a wooded col. Soon you make a steep climb into the open again among rock slabs and alpine vegetation. All at once you hear voices and find yourself among people at the junction with the Rim Trail from the Tramway. A large sign names the peaks in the panorama. A short trail leads to the summit, and an observation tower puts you above the spruces. The Tramway terminal hugs a niche, where ski trails begin to dive down.

Joining tourists at the tower, you look down the Notch and for an instant you are puzzled by a ribbon in the forest and toy cars. Across this highway,

Cannon Mountain

Continue down a rough stretch into less precipitous woods. Keep left past the Dodge Cutoff to Lonesome Lake. Hi-Cannon's switchbacks take you down to the Lonesome Lake Trail. Turn left and walk this graded path to Lafayette Campground. There, turn left and take the road out of the campground past the recreational building, Lafayette Lodge.

Follow the Profile Lake Trail that begins at the left just before the bridge out to the parking area. You have an interesting 2-mile hike north through the woods to the lake below the Profile. The mostly level trail crosses the Pemigewasset River on footbridges. Beavers have easily dammed the water, for it is only a brook, but they are gone now, and you can observe close at hand their gnawing technique on stumps. The trail rises to the lake. Keep left around the west side to the viewpoint for the Profile. Then walk north to the parking area and US 3, ¼ mile, and turn left into Profile Clearing where you parked your car.

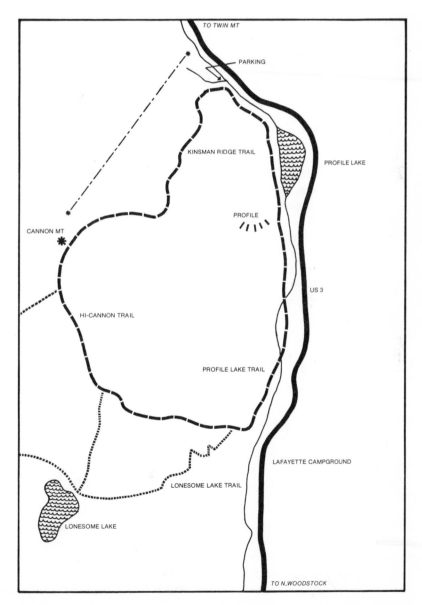

Cannon Mountain

Mount Kinsman has two summits. A wooded col and 1 mile of the Kinsman Ridge Trail connect them. The mountain forms a divide that separates the Merrimack River tributaries from the Connecticut River watershed to the west.

The north peak, elevation 4,275 feet, drops away 500 feet to narrow Kinsman Pond and the roof of the shelter near the spruce-grown shore. Beyond to the east, Lonesome Lake sparkles in the evergreen forest above Franconia Notch. Mount Lafayette, the giant of the region, rises across the Notch.

The south peak's dome, elevation 4,363 feet, because of topography and exposure, extends into the alpine-tundra zone above treeline, and provides views in all directions. From both summits, the Franconia Range outlines the eastern horizon. Sun and clouds endlessly shift lighting effects across the slopes.

Although hikers most often climb Mount Kinsman from Lonesome Lake, the route here described has the advantage of being less traveled and quite

removed from the popularity of the Franconia Notch area. This hike takes you over both peaks and returns you by the same route. The Mount Kinsman Trail begins from the west in Easton, a township now grown back to woods from family farms of the nineteenth century. The Mount Kinsman Trail climbs to the Kinsman Ridge Trail, which traverses both summits.

Easton's settlement began at the conclusion of the Revolution. About 1783, Nathan Kinsman cut the first narrow woodstrack into the wilderness territory that is now Easton. He brought in tools and supplies on six mules. He built a log cabin on his grant of six hundred acres. More settlers followed.

As in other mountain towns, the small meadows of Easton's valley and its rocky pastures fed and clothed an increasing population for seventy-five years until the Civil War. Then war casualties, hopes of easier western land, and cash wages from city industry drained away the young men. Now, along NH 116, trees grow tall

in the old farmland. The Mount Kinsman Trail crosses through some of this earlier farmland as it approaches the mountain's broad west slope. The trail begins on the east side of NH 116 seven miles north of Bungay Corner (on NH 112 west of Kinsman Notch). From the village of Franconia, the trail is 4 miles south on NH 116. Watch the mileage and go slowly or you'll miss the Forest Service trail sign at the entrance road. Turn in and drive in low gear about $\frac{1}{10}$ mile to an opening in the bushes for parking.

The trail follows a bulldozed logging road through sandy cuts. It is badly washed out in places, and bordered by young spruces and birches growing up in the old pastures. The road becomes a wide path through a stand of maples near the site of an old sugar house.

Climbing more steeply, you approach a brook after 1½ miles. To the left up a slope is the Kinsman Cabin of the White Mountain National Forest. A neglected relic of the era of

Mt. Kinsman, from Mt. Lafayette

Mount Kinsman

26. Mount Kinsman

Distance (round trip): 10 miles.
Walking time: 8 hours.
Vertical rise: 3,400 feet.

log cabins and shelters, the axemanship it displays makes it an irreplaceable antique.

Cross the brook, bearing right, and climb up a steeper logging road. You will soon step over another brook with a mossy ledge on the left, then Flume Brook. A branch trail leads down to a ravine and cascade. Shortly beyond Flume Brook, the main trail turns sharply left. A branch trail to the right leads to Bald Peak ¼ mile

through woods to wide views from rocks and blueberry bushes.

The main trail follows the dwindling brook. You look up at the steep ridge ahead. The trail rises steadily through spruces and firs. Golden-crowned kinglets, feeding in the upper branches, give notice of their presence only by faint cheeping notes and by small flutterings. But, if you look behind you on the steeper pitches, you can see the tiny

birds in the treetops level with your eyes.

Among stunted evergreens you reach the Kinsman Ridge Trail. (This trail is a long, 16-mile trek over Cannon Mountain and Mount Kinsman to Kinsman Notch.) Turn right, south, on the Kinsman Ridge Trail. Take note of this junction so you'll recognize it on your return. The Kinsman Ridge Trail, along here, makes a narrow passage through evergreens and leads

Mount Kinsman

over rocky ledges to the north peak.

The north summit is partially wooded yet it offers a sudden view of Mount Lafayette, which becomes breathtaking from the cliff reached by a short trail left, east, down among rocks and spruces. The jagged Franconia Range cuts across the eastern horizon.

To continue, climb back up the spur trail to the Kinsman Ridge Trail. Turn left and continue south. You descend to the col and climb up out of the evergreens to the bare south dome and the summit cairn.

On several acres of open rock and dwarf spruces trimmed by the wind, you wander among abundant mountain plants, lichens, mosses, sedges, and grasses. In places, a matted turf has formed, held down by the roots of dwarf blueberry, Labrador tea, and mountain cranberry. Cool breezes and fine views make this the hike's ideal lunch setting.

In the afternoon, go back north along the Kinsman Ridge Trail over the north peak. Watch for the left turn into

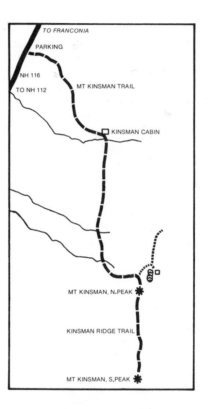

the Mount Kinsman Trail; it's easy to miss. Proceed down the Mount Kinsman Trail. Follow the route of your ascent, and remember not to be fooled at the corner where the Bald Peak spur trail invites you straight ahead; turn sharply right, down the straight logging road, then bear left across the brook before the Kinsman Cabin, and on down to your car.

Mount Kinsman

27. Mount Moosilauke

Distance (round trip): 6 miles.
Walking time: 4½ hours.
Vertical rise: 2,400 feet.

Rime ice

Rise early for Mount Moosilauke. It's a destination and an event. Bulking large on the southwestern border of the mountains, elevation 4,810 feet, massive and alone, its bare summit commands wide views in a complete circle.

The Franconias, fourteen miles northeast, march across the horizon. Far beyond them, Mount Washington appears with other Presidential peaks. More to the east, Mount Carrigain stands sentinel at the eastern approach to the Pemigewasset "Wilderness," which is bordered on the south by Mount Hancock, Osceola, Tripyramid, and the Sandwich Range. Directly south, smaller mountains scattered in the foothills blend toward isolated Mount Kearsarge (South) and Mount Cardigan. Westward, across the verdant Connecticut valley, Vermont's Green Mountains extend as far as Killington Peak, Mount Mansfield, and Jay Peak.

Mount Moosilauke has been popular for more than a hundred years. In 1860, Sam Hoit built his stone Prospect House on the windswept summit. The opening ceremonies on the Fourth of July, according to one authority, attracted a thousand men and women. The gala crowd included a brass band, orators, militia, and Indians. Refreshments were served. The Carriage Road continued to bring guests from Warren.

The Carriage Road was still safe for horse-drawn rigs in 1917. Dartmouth College took over the hotel in 1920 and put in bunks and accommodations for eighty hikers. In the summer, students managed the Summit House, or Tip-Top House as it was then called. Moosilauke has remained Dartmouth's mountain, although the Summit House burned in 1942. A new cabin, aluminum with diagonal orange stripes, serves

Mount Moosilauke

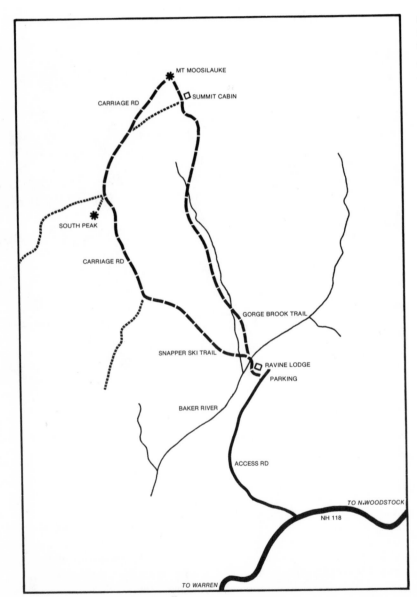

as an emergency shelter 400 feet south of the summit. The college land is maintained as a wilderness area free from motor vehicles, where overnight camping and open fires are not permitted. This policy of limited use is designed to protect the unique and fragile mountain environment.

At all times the mountain can be cold and icy. Gales sweep down upon it with dangerous speed and intensity. Above treeline, clouds often shroud the rocks. The south shoulder, 1 mile long, is exposed to storms, and on a gloomy day suggests the beginning of the world despite the trail along the old Carriage Road traversing its length.

The trails starting near Dartmouth's Ravine Lodge offer the widest selection and most spectacular routes. Turn west off NH 118 between Warren and North Woodstock, 6 miles from Warren, onto the access road to the Lodge. Park at the end of the right fork above the Lodge.

Mount Moosilauke

The Gorge Brook Trail begins on the west side of Baker River across a footbridge in front of the Lodge. Turn left along a path on the west bank a short distance, then right onto Gorge Brook Trail. After ¼ mile the Snapper Ski Trail branches left and offers an alternate or return route. The Gorge Brook Trail is more direct, rising steadily toward the summit. It follows an old logging road through mixed growths of hardwoods and spruces beside Gorge Brook's pools and cascades. The trail crosses Gorge Brook twice before the steepest section about 1 mile from the start. A trail up Gorge Brook Slide diverges left to the Carriage Road. The main Gorge Brook Trail continues steeply upward through spruce/fir woods, some of the 3,000-foot bird, the blackpoll warbler.

Approaching treeline, the trail becomes more gradual, and the views begin to open up. Scrubby heaths alternate with twisted spruces around the emergency cabin and the spring. The trail, marked by cairns, continues northerly to the summit ledges, the rectangular stone foundations that once supported the Summit House, and the encompassing panorama.

To descend by the Snapper Ski Trail, take the Carriage Road south along the rocky ridge. If this is hidden in cloud, return to the cabin and turn right, into the scrub on a section of the Appalachian Trail, which passes little mountain meadows and joins the Carriage Road where it is easier to follow in fog. (If a storm threatens while you are on the summit, return by the Gorge Brook Trail.) About 1 mile south of the summit on the Carriage Road, the Glencliff Trail, a link in the route the Appalachian Trail follows to Hanover and on into Vermont, drops down into the woods, right.

Just beyond the Glencliff Trail, a short spur leads west to the south peak for a view of the forested Baker River valley, Lake Tarleton, Mount Cube, Smarts Mountain, and various ponds.

Keep on the Carriage Road for 1 mile, passing the Gorge Brook Slide Trail on the left, and descending the rocky, washed-out track to the Snapper Ski Trail, where you turn left. This is now a footpath with views over steep drops. The loop is completed down at Gorge Brook Trail, about 1 mile.

Mount Moosilauke

View of Mt. Garfield

Mount Garfield's rocky summit commands a spectacular and unique view across a northern valley of the Pemigewasset "Wilderness." Due south from Mount Garfield, Owl's Head—itself a 4,023-foot mountain—blocks the valley and forces Franconia Brook east, while forming a narrow gap below the Franconia Range. There, on the west, Mounts Lafayette and Lincoln rise to a heavy, peaked ridge. Mount Liberty stands alone, and Flume's spire farther south has its separate identity.

You look east down to AMC's Garfield Ridge Campsites and Shelter. Away off in that direction, Galehead Hut appears as a toy building among miles of evergreens. A line of summits shapes the eastern horizon and extends southward from North Twin over South Twin, Zealand Mountain, Guyot, and Bond to Bondcliff in the Pemigewasset River's East Branch valley.

The Garfield Trail approaches the mountain from US 3 and takes you up the long western slope to the steep cone, at 4,488 feet.

Mount Garfield

28. Mount Garfield

Distance (round trip): 10 miles.
Walking time: 6 hours.
Vertical rise: 3,100 feet.

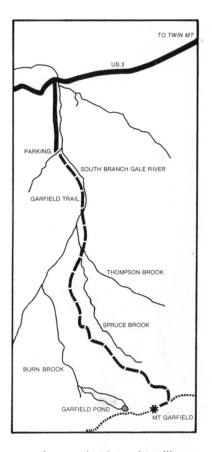

Drive north through Franconia Notch on US 3. At the Interstate 93 junction, keep right, toward Twin Mountain, 5 miles. There's a wide turnout, right, before the bridge over Gale River. Take the Forest Service road leaving the turnout left, and follow it about ½ mile to a designated parking space, left. Walk straight up the road past a bridge, left, and along a rough logging road up the west side of Gale River's South Branch. After ½ mile, the Garfield Trail turns left across the brook, and the logging road bears right.

The trail leads up gradually, through fine woods to crossings at Thompson and Spruce Brooks. (Last sure water.) The good walking continues. This is one of the pleasantest trails in the mountains, but, for years after a forest fire in 1902, the trail traversed burned country. As often happens in logged and burned land, birches took over. Now their white trunks shine in sunlight along the trail.

After a short downhill grade below a ledgy bank, left, the trail climbs the steeper slope by long inclines between switchback turns. The birches yield to spruce/fir woods higher up. When you are 4½ miles from the road, you pass the former Garfield Pond Cutoff on the right. Keep left. (The Garfield Pond Cutoff has been closed and the shelter taken down to allow the closed area to recover from too much camping.)

The Garfield Trail, steadily rising, joins the Garfield Ridge Trail after ¼ mile. (The Garfield Ridge Trail comes up at the left from the Garfield Ridge Campsites.) Follow this joint trail to the right, up toward the summit. You climb a steep pitch up through rocks and spruces for another ¼ mile. At the crest, turn left. It's 50 yards to the summit rocks and a former tower's concrete foundation. (Garfield Ridge Trail continues to Mount Lafayette.)

In August 1907, Mount Garfield overlooked a holocaust. Twenty-five thousand acres, left in slash by J. E. Henry's logging, burst into flame as lightning struck the east side of Owl's Head. This fire was one of many that brought militant attention to the desolation caused by lumbermen, and led to the Weeks Bill of 1911 that established the White Mountain National Forest.

There's no loop to this hike. Return by the same route you came.

Mount Garfield

Tripoli Road, Breadtray Ridge, Thornton Gap, Scar Ridge, Mad River—these colorful names from loggers' parlance enliven maps of the country that surrounds this peak named for the famous Seminole warrior. Mount Osceola dominates the upper end of Waterville Valley. Its 4,326-foot elevation viewed from the west appears as a single summit, but, seen from the east along the Kancamagus Highway, the East Peak's 4,185-foot shoulder enlarges the mountain.

The most direct trail to the main summit begins at Waterville Valley's northwest pass, Thornton Gap. From Campton drive east on NH 49, 10 miles up the Mad River. Turn left, and drive past the access road to Tecumseh Ski Area. This Tripoli Road crests 4½ miles from NH 49 at the 2,300-foot pass. About 200 yards beyond, the Mount Osceola Trail enters the woods on the right (north). Park opposite along the roadside.

On Mt. Osceola

Mount Osceola

29. Mount Osceola

Distance (Tripoli Road to main peak and return): 7 miles.
Walking time: 4½ hours.
Vertical rise: 2,025 feet.

Through second-growth cherry and poplar trees, you climb an old tractor road to a stony section between young white birches. The trail becomes a series of gravel switchbacks. You look off to Mount Tripyramid's North Slide. More switchbacks take you up Breadtray Ridge to views of Mount Tecumseh's ski trails and Sandwich Mountain to the south beyond the green Waterville Valley. At a log-bridged gully, you stop at a spring, left, among spruces at the head of a little brook. Climbing again, you walk over log steps that prevent washouts, swing left more steeply, then right and left several times, and pass another spring on your right. Near the top of the ridge, the trail turns sharply right, east, and leads up to the level approach through summit spruces to the ledges and tower.

You now stand on the highest of the mountains encircling Waterville Valley. Slightly south of east, Mount Tripyramid's three peaks notch the horizon five miles away. An unusual nearby view extends north into the valley along Hancock

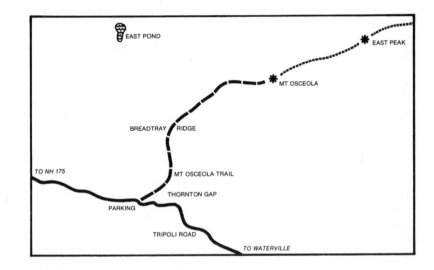

Branch and the Kancamagus Highway. On the right of Mount Hancock, and more distant, Mount Carrigain's angular bulk gives you a line on Mount Washington, twenty-two miles away. Turning northwest, you can orient yourself by the sentinel, Mount Garfield, and find to your left Mounts Lafayette and Lincoln. Of the remaining Franconias, Mounts Liberty and Flume are pinnacles in the direction of Cannon Mountain. More to the west, Kinsman's north and south summits appear as a ridge, but Mount Moosilauke stands out as the important western peak.

Return to Tripoli Road by the route of ascent.

Those hardy souls who yearn to climb all the accepted 4,000-foot peaks will continue east on the Mount Osceola Trail, and will think nothing of the descent and climb to East Peak 1 mile away. They may even keep on down the steep and hazardous trail to Greeley Ponds and out to the Kancamagus Highway for a total of 7 miles from the Tripoli Road. (See hike number 9.) This exploit requires 2 more hours than Osceola alone, and arrangement for transportation at the end.

Mount Osceola

The name describes the three peaks; it says nothing about the two slides. For pure joy in climbing, the North Slide is hard to beat. You choose your own way over the angular ledges. There is little danger in dry weather. A wild and extensive view opens behind you. The trees fall away, the world seems to enlarge in scope and promise. The rocks, which appeared so formidable from below, now offer a clear way skyward. You are conquering the mountain.

From the Livermore Road out of Waterville Valley, you hike a loop up the exciting North Slide, over the three peaks, down the treacherous South Slide, and back to the road.

The slides tore out the woods and rocks on both North and South Peaks in 1885; they were forecast by an earlier slide that scarred South Peak sixteen years before. The slides are completely unlike, the North Slide being ledges, the South Slide rocks and gravel. The three peaks rise in a line from a ridge about 1 mile long.

North Peak's elevation is 4,140 feet. Middle Peak reaches to

Trail signs on Mt. Tripyramid

4,110 feet. South Peak crests at 4,090 feet.

From Campton, drive east on NH 49, 10 miles up the Mad River. Turn left and drive past the access road to Tecumseh Ski Area. About 2 miles from NH 49, turn right across the Mad River's West Branch. Keep left at a fork just beyond the bridge. Drive almost ½ mile, crossing a clearing known as Depot Camp. Continue over a small bridge to another fork. Your route is to the right up

the Forest Service's Livermore Road, which is closed to cars from this junction. (The left fork leads to the Greeley Ponds Trail.) Park clear of the road.

Walk up the Livermore Road about 2 miles. The trail to South Slide begins on the right. (You will return this way after your loop over Tripyramid.) Keep on the road another 1 mile. Before a sharp left bend

Mount Tripyramid

30. Mount Tripyramid

Distance (round trip): 10½ miles.
Walking time: 7 hours.
Vertical rise (including all three peaks): 3,050 feet.

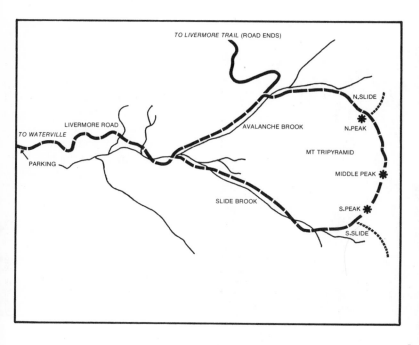

To proceed on the trail from North Peak, face away from the view. Joining from the left, Pine Bend Brook Trail (from the Kancamagus Highway) becomes the trail south down the ridge. It ends after ½ mile at the Sabbaday Brook Trail, left (from the Kancamagus Highway). You keep straight along and begin the climb up and over Middle Peak, then South Peak. Descending, you come to the South Slide and to forested vistas stretching away west. The two Flat Mountain Ponds lie in a hollow left of Sandwich Mountain. Ski trails identify Mount Tecumseh. Mount Moosilauke dominates the western horizon.

About halfway down the slide at a sign and cairn, the Sleeper Trail comes in on your left from Mount Whiteface. Keep on down the slide. Watch for rolling gravel and loose rocks as you place your feet. At the base of the slide, bear right. The trail enters the woods and runs above Slide Brook to a crossing over Avalanche Brook and the terminus at the Livermore Road. Turn left down the road for the return to your car.

at a switchback, the trail to North Slide drops off the road to the right and crosses Avalanche Brook.

The trail follows a former logging road ¾ mile to the base of the slide. The brook offers the last water; there is no water on the mountain. Climb the slide as you will. You can't go wrong if you keep scrambling up, although you should bear right near the top, for the trail enters the spruces at the upper left corner of the west sec-

tion, which is on your right.

The short remaining climb in the woods takes you to the North Peak and open ledges with a tremendous 180-degree view starting in the west and swinging northwest to include the Franconia Range and farther around to Mount Washington, northeast—all from a rare angle across the Kancamagus Highway and over the forests of the Pemigewasset "Wilderness."

Mount Tripyramid

The roadless upper watershed of the Pemigewasset River's East Branch separates Franconia Notch and Crawford Notch and their adjacent mountains. The main highways circle this country and leave the tourist unaware of the forested valleys and peaks between the two sections of the White Mountains. A hike to Zeacliff fills this vacancy.

You approach this great outlook along an abandoned railroad grade once used to haul logs out to the mills. The grade parallels the Zealand River toward its source. Beavers dam the branching streams. Zealand Pond, at the end of swampy meadows, has two outlets. Mid-June is a fine time to walk the Zealand Trail and look for birds. At that time, too, the rhodora blooms pink across the bogs.

Perched above the pond, AMC's Zealand Falls Hut offers accommodations to thirty-six hikers and a view directly to Mount Carrigain.

Near Zeacliff

Between the Notches: Zeacliff

31. Between the Notches: Zeacliff

Distance (round trip via Twinway): 7½ miles.
(round trip, including loop through Zeland Notch): 9¼ miles.
Walking time (via Twinway): 4½ hours.
(through Zealand Notch): 6½ hours.
Vertical rise: 1,500 feet.

Zeacliff is about 1 mile above by the Twinway, a mountain trail. This steady climb brings you to Zeacliff's lookoff ledge above wooded valleys and mountains stretching away south and east, with views of Zealand Notch and Whitewall Mountain, both seared by fire during and after the logging days of the 1880s and early 1900s. This old, slashed and burned country has grown up largely to hardwoods. Former logging roads appear as green ribbons along distant contours of lighter growth. Sometimes ravens hover over the cliffs.

To reach the beginning of the Zealand Trail and the railroad grade, drive to Zealand Campground on US 302 about 2½ miles east from Twin Mountain. Turn south on the Forest Service's Zealand Road, which crosses the Ammonoosuc River and leads up a steep hill to a steadily ascending valley. Pass the Sugarloaf Camping Area and continue to the Zealand Road's end, 3½ miles from the highway.

The Zealand Trail takes off beyond a small brook crossing. It follows the railroad grade except for short sections cut through the woods where the railroad once crossed Zealand River for short distances. In this way the trail keeps west of the dwindling river, which divides into its source streams. You approach Zealand Pond through a boggy country of meadows and beaver ponds.

About 2 miles from the start of the Zealand Trail, the A-Z Trail enters from the left. (The A-Z Trail connects to trails from the Crawford House and Crawford Notch's Willey Range.) You cross the north outlet of Zealand Pond and follow the east shore. At the south end, where you make a sharp right turn, the Ethan Pond Trail enters from the left. (The Ethan Pond Trail leads through Zealand Notch.) Keep right, across a wet section at the south outlet of Zealand Pond. Soon you climb the trail's only steep rise to its terminus at the Zealand Falls Hut, 2,700 feet elevation.

Behind the Hut, take the Twinway Trail up past the Lend-a-Hand Trail at the right. (The Lend-a-Hand Trail climbs Mount Hale.) Cross the small brook above the falls. Here is the last water. The Twinway Trail is rough and steep compared to the previous railroad grade. White birches grow smaller as the trail climbs into stunted spruces. It emerges on the rocky summit of the ridge leading toward Zealand Mountain, Mount Guyot, and South Twin. At an unmarked fork in the trail just before the summit rocks, bear left for the top of Zeacliff, which is on a short loop off the main Twinway Trail. The cliff overlooks Zealand Notch and faces Whitewall Mountain.

You are looking across the Forest Service's Lincoln Woods Scenic Area, which consists of 18,560 acres preserved in their wildness. Mount Carrigain towers across the forest. Ponds draining into the Pemigewasset River's East Branch glisten in the valleys. To the left of Carrigain you sight through Carrigain Notch next to Mount Lowell. To the right of Carrigain, Mount Hancock is a solid outline. Closer and to the west, Mount Bond reaches away south from its barren crown.

If you are in shape for a tough and dramatic descent, part of your return may be made by a different trail. Walk west along the Twinway a short distance to the Zeacliff Trail, left. Turn down this steep, rough way that leads under the cliffs and down an old slide into the valley where Whitewall Brook runs through Zealand Notch. Then a brief climb takes you up to the Ethan Pond Trail. Turn left, north, for the hike back to Zealand Pond along the old railroad grade. This loop is a distance of 3 miles as compared to the 1¼ miles back the way you came from Zealand Falls Hut. But it's an experience passing through Zealand Notch before hiking out to your car.

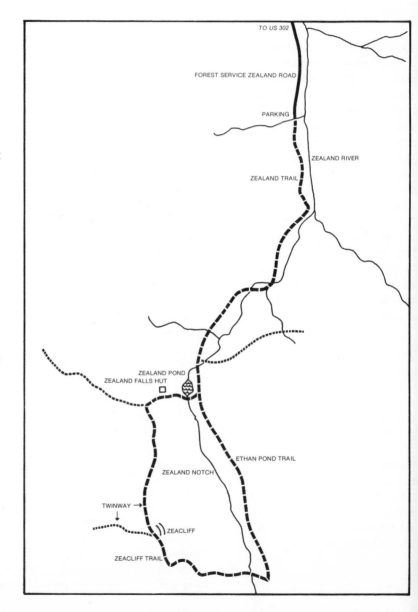

Between the Notches: Zeacliff

Mount Washington Region

Pinkham Notch appears less spectacular near the highway than either Franconia or Crawford Notch. But, situated close under Mount Washington's eastern ravines, Pinkham Notch has its own distinction: it's a climbing center. It's as near as you can drive on a main highway (NH 16) to the most impressive mountain in New England—Mount Washington. Major trails pass through or start in Pinkham Notch. It's the mountain climbers' base, a takeoff for the Presidential Range.

Pinkham Notch has changed since 1826, when Daniel Pinkham built the road through his grant between Jackson and Randolph. Now there's the wide highway: traffic on NH 16 would astound Daniel Pinkham. The AMC Pinkham Notch Camp (10 miles north of Jackson), established in 1920, has outgrown the original log cabins and has become a complex, modern headquarters for the AMC Huts and Trail System, with plentiful parking and accommodations for a hundred

Pinkham Notch Camp

Pinkham Notch: the Crew-Cut Trail

32. Pinkham Notch: The Crew-Cut Trail

Distance (round trip): 1¾ miles.
Walking time: 1¼ hours.
Vertical rise: 400 feet.

guests. At Wildcat Ski Area the gondola lift operates year round.

As part of an introductory hike, the 1-mile Crew-Cut Trail winds through hardwood forest to a lookout ledge at the north end of Pinkham Notch. To start the hike, turn west off NH 16 at Pinkham Notch Camp. Park along the old road. Walk past the lodge toward Mount Washington. Turn right to the Tuckerman Ravine Trail. About 300 feet past the buildings on the right, watch for the sign to the Old Jackson Road. Bear right on this trail. Cross a work road, following the yellow disks on trees. The trail winds through open woods ¼ mile to a junction where the unused section of the Old Jackson Road comes in from the highway. A few yards to the left along the road, the Crew-Cut Trail branches right. Follow the red paint blazes across a seasonal brook and swing left. Poorly marked for a distance, the trail makes a right turn.

The trail requires attention if it is to be followed through this section among beech and

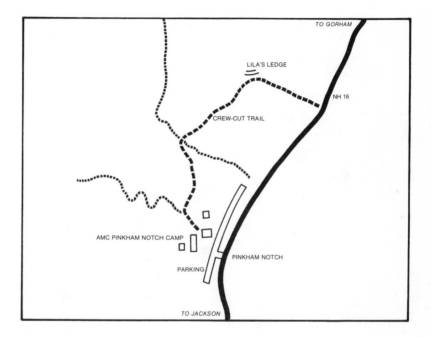

yellow birch trees. Across the second brook, keep straight past the George's Gorge Trail, left. Orange paint blazes supplement the older red blazes. The trail climbs over a knoll and enters an area of broken ledges under the tall trees as it approaches the base of a cliff. The main trail turns sharply right. A spur trail leads straight to the lookout called Lila's Ledge. This pinnacle offers a view from its lower corner toward Wildcat Ski Area. Above, for the experi-

enced and agile climber, a wide view opens into Pinkham Notch and up to Mount Washington.

The main trail, avoiding the cliff, curves left and goes down steeply across several levels of the slope. It passes through the seepage from a small bog shortly before reaching NH 16, 50 yards south and opposite the ski area's parking lot.

Return to your car by the same route you came.

Treeline warning sign, Mt. Washington.

The half-day excursion from Pinkham Notch to Lowe's Bald Spot takes you to a 3,000-foot opening on Mount Washington's eastern slope. By easy trails you experience the mountain's sweep and primitive power. You look away to the peaks north and west. Wide views open east to the Carter Range and south through Pinkham Notch. Lowe's Bald Spot gives you mountain air and sunlight, distant skies and the near scent of fir balsam. You may even forget asphalt highways, cars, cities, and mortgage payments.

Turn off NH 16 for parking at the AMC Pinkham Notch Camp. Beyond the lodge take the Tuckerman Ravine Trail 100 yards to the branch trail right, leading to the Old Jackson Road. The trail crosses through hardwoods to the ancient road, which is now a trail. It rises 600 feet during the 1½ miles before it brings you to the Mount Washington Automobile Road, still known as the Carriage Road from its original use more than a hundred years ago.

Lowe's Bald Spot

33. Lowe's Bald Spot

Distance (round trip): 4¼ miles.
Walking time: 2¾ hours.
Vertical rise: 1,000 feet.

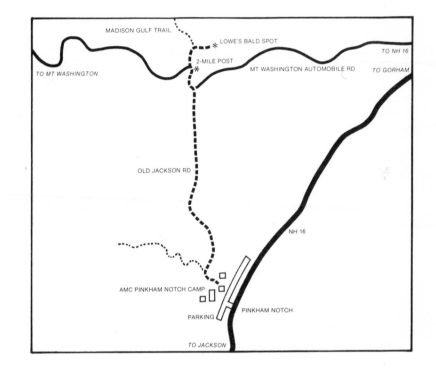

After you enter the auto road, keep on, straight ahead and uphill, and pass two trails on your left: the Raymond Path to Tuckerman Ravine and the Nelson Crag Trail. Continue up the auto road to the two-mile marker, which indicates the distance from the road's beginning at NH 16. Watch for a trail to the right leading into the evergreens. You are looking for the Madison Gulf Trail but vandalism has forced trail crews to move the signs away from the auto road; they are now along the trails about 100 feet from the road.

Follow the Madison Gulf Trail ¼ mile to a branch trail, right, and the short climb to Lowe's Bald Spot. (The Madison Gulf Trail continues to the Great Gulf, up to tree-line, and to the AMC Madison Hut in the barren col between Mount Adams and Mount Madison, the northeastern pinnacle of the Presidential Range. The Trail is also a link to the Great Gulf Trail, the shelters, and the trails leaving the Gulf for the high peaks. The entire Madison Gulf Trail takes 5 hours of steady hiking and strenuous climbing up the steep headwall of Madison Gulf.)

After the short climb from the main trail to Lowe's Bald Spot, you look north across the lower valley of the Great Gulf and the West Branch of the Peabody River to Mount Adams and Mount Madison. West is the headwall of Huntington Ravine topped by Nelson Crag and the bare cone of Mount Washington, a desert of jumbled stones rising in unforgettable contrast to the green trees below. Up there, earth's verdure emerges miraculously from its mineral source. Yet the grim environment might suggest to you an atomic blast's rubble. If it does, you are happy to hear the birds singing in the nearby spruces and to see hikers on the trails, and almost relieved to hear autos grinding up the road.

West of the highway (NH 16) through Pinkham Notch and about 8 miles north of Jackson, a high bare ridge supports Glen Boulder among lesser rocks. Outlined against the sky, the great boulder appears about to topple into the Notch.

A climb to this landmark also lifts you rapidly to treeline with its strange ecology of ledge and lichen. Glen Boulder is a good destination for an afternoon. Besides being the shortest route to treeline on this eastern side of Mount Washington, it tests your legs and offers a superb panorama of mountainous slopes, valleys, and summits.

The Glen Boulder Trail, cut and marked in 1905, leaves the parking circle and picnic sites at Glen Ellis Falls on the west side of NH 16, 9 miles north of Jackson. (Glen Ellis Falls, reached by a tunnel under the highway and by stone steps into a ravine, sluice spectacularly from a ledge seventy feet into a rocky pool. The water of Ellis River pours out as from a pitcher. Mist cools the air blowing across the evergreens and the pool, where

Glen Boulder

sightseers click cameras.) The Glen Boulder Trail, rising from the parking area's south corner, slabs across a steep service road and swings right, climbing to level woods. Here you pass through a typical 2,000-foot hardwood forest. Big yellow birches, beeches, and other deciduous trees shade striped maples, hobble bushes, and ferns. Wood thrushes and hermit thrushes inhabit the ground and undergrowth.

At the second steep pitch, which takes you to the base of a cliff, the trail divides. The right fork avoids a rough chimney. Both trails leads to the continuation of the main trail above the cliff. Beyond this, a spur trail, left, leads to a view up the Notch and across to Wildcat Mountain. The main trail soon begins a steep ascent. After ½ hour of steady climbing, you cross a

Glen Boulder

34. Glen Boulder

Distance (to Glen Boulder and back): 3 miles.
Walking time: 3 hours.
Vertical rise: 1,800 feet.

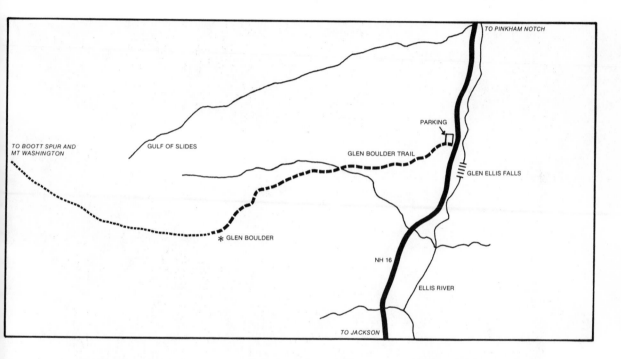

brook and approach the abruptly rising shoulder up which you climb from treeline ¼ mile to Glen Boulder.

Facing south you look away twenty miles to Mount Chocorua's rocky tower. The sweep is to your left over the Saco River and Ellis River valleys to nearby Wildcat Ridge and around over Pinkham Notch to Mount Washington.

The Glen Boulder Trail continues steeply above treeline

and through scrub spruce for more than 1½ miles to the Davis Path. This fine route to Mount Washington should be undertaken only by seasoned climbers. From Glen Boulder to Mount Washington's summit via the Davis Path and the Crawford Path is a rugged, long 4 miles. A loop to the AMC Lakes-of-the-Clouds Hut adds another 1 mile. These trails are more difficult than they appear and take longer than you might estimate; allow 3 hours

of constant walking and climbing, at least, even in good weather. If there's any sign of clouds descending, rain, or storm, turn around at the boulder and descend to your car.

This is also a warning to the beginner and to the exhilarated devotee who want to go on just a while longer. You planned a short climb to Glen Boulder. Enjoy yourself there, then head back.

Glen Boulder

Tuckerman Ravine

35. Tuckerman Ravine

Distance (to the Snow Arch and back): 6¼ miles.
Walking time: 5 hours.
Vertical rise: 2,300 feet.

A glacial cirque of rocks and cliffs gouged at treeline by prehistoric ice, this dramatic basin in Mount Washington's southeast slope can be an exciting destination as well as the beginning of the strenuous upper climbing to the summit. Open-front shelters amid spruces surround little Hermit Lake. The headwall's precipices are famous for spring skiing when they are banked by tremendous snow accumulations; they drip veils of water that gather at the base to undercut the remaining snow and form the Snow Arch, which survives well into summer.

On the north, the cliff named Lion Head juts into the Ravine toward the south wall, which is crowned by Boott Spur. East, from the open half-basin, the view extends across Pinkham Notch to Wildcat Ridge and the Carter Range. Climbing directly from the Notch into this giant amphitheater, the Tuckerman Ravine Trail follows a graded tractor path 2½ miles up to Hermit Lake and the shelters.

Tuckerman Ravine Headwall

Drive north from Jackson on NH 16 for 10 miles until you come to a large sign on the west side identifying the AMC Pinkham Notch Camp. Turn in and leave your car in the long parking strip, where other hikers, young and old, are preparing to leave for the trails or are returning. Here at the AMC lodge you'll find information on the trails, a snack bar, and other facilities. (Here also you may obtain the permit required if you plan to stay overnight in the Ravine's shelters.)

To reach the Tuckerman Ravine Trail, walk past the main lodge and turn right. Keep to the wide tractor path. It presents good footing and equable grades suitable for all hikers regardless of experience or ability; but it's still an uphill climb and hikers intending to climb above treeline should take to heart the warning sign about adequate clothing and food and good physical condition.

The path crosses Cutler River, named soon after the Revolution for an explorer, the Reverend Manasseh Cut-

ler. His party changed the mountain's name from Agiochook to Washington. Beyond the footbridge over this stream whose source is far up under the headwall, you turn a right corner and begin to climb. Soon, on the right again, take a few steps up to a ledge across from Crystal Cascade, one of the most impressive in the mountains.

The path continues to climb by easy switchbacks through a forest of big yellow birch and beech. These woods are favored by the winter wren, in summer only, despite his name. He's notable for his small size and for his vertical tailfeathers. You hear his voluble song more often than you see him in the underbrush.

After about 1 mile, the woods change to spruce and fir interspersed with white birch and mountain ash. You may expect to catch glimpses of boreal chickadees in the evergreens. Their brown caps differentiate them from the common black-capped chickadees. The boreals sing a husky series of notes lacking one

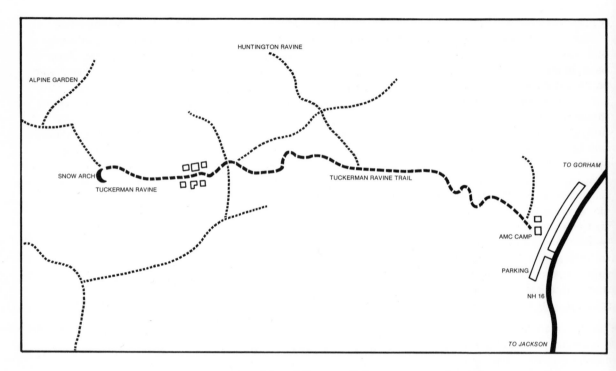

ALPINE GARDEN

HUNTINGTON RAVINE

SNOW ARCH

TUCKERMAN RAVINE

TUCKERMAN RAVINE TRAIL

TO GORHAM

AMC CAMP

PARKING

NH 16

TO JACKSON

or two "dees." Rare until the last few years, they seem to have discovered and taken over the cool White Mountains, which lie south of their regular habitat.

Along the Tuckerman Ravine Trail, access links to the John Sherburne Ski Trail occur at intervals on the left. These are marked by signs and can be easily avoided. Stay on the graded tractor path. Continue past the Hun-

tington Ravine Trail, which branches right. Cross a wooden bridge over the Cutler River, where hikers often rest and admire the view toward Wildcat Ridge.

Two miles of steady climbing take you past the Raymond Path on the right and around a wide S-turn into the Ravine. You pass the Lion Head Trail, right, and the Boott Spur link on the left. The Ravine opens up to the wide

Tuckerman Ravine

sky and bare rocks. The shelters appear along side trails and across Hermit Lake. (The central building, known as "Howard Johnson's," burned in the spring of 1972. The name, applied satirically years ago to an earlier building that also burned, expressed the attitude of various salty characters who preferred the primitive Ravine when it had only two log shelters.) Cliffs tower above, and, to the west, beyond a rocky slope edged with scrub spruce, the headwall rises perpendicularly toward the clouds that coast steadily eastward.

The open-front shelters are for the eighty-six overnight hikers who obtain permits at the Pinkham Notch Camp. Overuse of the limited area, as throughout the mountains at certain popular spots, has made new regulations necessary. Camping in the woods has been discontinued to preserve the delicate subalpine soil, trees, and plant life. Hikers should bring their own lunches and carry out their own trash. If cooking is planned, they should carry portable stoves; wood or char-

coal fires are not allowed. The endangered ecology is responding to these conservation measures; hikers realize the problem and help.

A ¾-mile climb over a trail now rough and rocky leads you to the headwall and the Snow Arch. (This is still Tuckerman Ravine Trail continuing from the shelter area on the north or right side of the brook.) Never walk under the Snow Arch. Huge chunks fall off without warning. By late summer it has melted away into Cutler River.

The Tuckerman Ravine Trail finds a route over rocks at the base of the cliffs, and circles the headwall to the north of the cliffs. Hikers on holiday weekends form a moving line of figures on the trail up and across the headwall. Balmy weather in the Ravine sometimes changes to icy wind and clouds above; plan on its doing so.

The summit of Mount Washington is only 1 mile from the Snow Arch, but it's a mile to remember. Time is a better measure: 2 hours, if you are accustomed to scrambling

over rocks at such an angle. The 1,000 feet up to the summit from the diverging trails above the headwall (known as Tuckerman Junction) appear less because above treeline there is no familiar sight for estimating distance. The landscape is as strange as the sudden storms are fierce. And the higher you climb the fiercer they get; the protection of the Ravine is often welcome.

Mount Washington

36. Mount Washington

Distance (round trip): 8 miles.
Walking time: 8 hours.
Vertical rise: 3,600 feet.

By its western approach, the route of this climb to Mount Washington takes you up the steep and scenic Ammonoosuc Ravine from the cog railway's Base Station. Just above tree-line, the AMC Lakes-of-the-Clouds Hut offers shelter if the weather turns frigid and stormy. Mount Washington's rocky cone and the summit buildings tower 1,200 feet higher and 1½ miles away at the top of the 150-year-old trail laid out by the legendary mountaineer, Ethan Allen Crawford.

On the summit, you'll meet tourists who came on the cog railway or in their cars. They think you are out of your mind for climbing when you could ride. For the dyed-in-the-wool hiker once or twice on the summit is enough, unforgettable as it is.

Save this climb for a day of matchless clarity, so rare on this peak of cloud, rain, and storm. Waiting for a clear day will prove worthwhile. Then the far horizon will be the limit of vision, and you'll see a great sweep of country that includes

Mt. Washington, from Mt. Jefferson

most of New Hampshire and parts of Maine, Vermont, and the Province of Quebec. You will stand at the center of a circle two hundred miles in diameter, enclosing hundreds of mountains and valleys in thirty thousand square miles. Perhaps you'll see the ocean to the east, blending with the sky.

Leave US 302 at Fabyan and drive on the Base Road 7½ miles to the cog railway's Base Station. At the bottom of the final hill before the parking area for passengers, turn right into the hikers' parking space. In the summer season an attendant collects the nominal fee (50¢ in 1972) and issues a car tag. Shoulder your pack. It should contain an insulated jacket, parka, cap, gloves, and a supply of emergency food as well as your lunch. If you climb in shorts, carry warm pants. You are heading for an arctic-alpine zone.

Those barren heights appear above you as you walk up the road to the station. Nearby, gala-clad vacationers watch engineers in overalls, grimy

firemen, and brakemen, or they visit the gift shop and snack bar while they await train time. Engines with tilted boilers puff smoke and steam from coal fires and push passenger cars up the steep track by means of a drive gear engaging the steel pins set between the two walls of a center rail. This was the invention of New Hampshire–born Sylvester Marsh. In 1869 President Ulysses S. Grant rode up the mountain on the first train, along with P. T. Barnum who allowed that the next morning's sunrise was the "second greatest show on earth."

The Ammonoosuc Ravine Trail starts behind cabins on a knoll to the south of the station. It leads you through woods as you follow the small Ammonoosuc River on your left for 1½ miles to a fine waterfall and pool.

Across the stream you begin the precipitous ascent up steps among spruces. The trail faces you like a rough, rocky wall of earth reinforced with tree roots. Part way up this first steep section, a spur trail on the right offers you the opportunity to see the brook's glittering torrent pour down a long stone sluice formed by ledges. Climbing on up the main trail, you pass wide carpets of green-leaved wood sorrel, which blooms white in mid-July. You come to another high falls where at this altitude the mountain or alpine avens bloom yellow in early July. Among open rocks, Labrador tea puts out white frilly flowers, and bog laurel shows pink blooms above moist turf.

Ten minutes climbing brings you to another falls and brook crossing, then soon to another. The spruces dwindle to the ancient dwarf clumps twisted and flattened by winds at treeline. The scrub growth ends at the vast expanse of rocks, which extends to Mount Washington's summit on your left. Follow cairns and yellow paint arrows the last 100 yards over the ledges to the Lakes-of-the-Clouds Hut on the windswept col between Mount Washington and Mount Monroe on your right.

This AMC hut is the largest (excluding the headquarters at Pinkham Notch Camp) in the nine-hut system. Stone walls first withstood the gales at 5,000 feet in 1915. Now expanded and modernized with a capacity of ninety guests, the Hut is a popular stopover. Many hikers cross from the Tuckerman Ravine Trail, descend from Mount Washington, or traverse the 7-mile ridge from Crawford Notch. The Hut is the terminus of the Ammonoosuc Ravine Trail.

Here the wind, and often clouds in the form of dense fog, as well as violent summer storms of rain, lightning, and sleet, decide for you whether or not you climb on toward the summit on this try. You will probably understand why unwary hikers above treeline on Mount Washington have perished from exposure in summer.

When the weather's favorable, take the Crawford Path from the Hut and follow it between the two little lakes whose stony shores and ledges support alpine plants, sedges, and shrubs. These botanical miracles possess the unbelievable tenacity of mountain flora as long as nature's delicate balance remains undisturbed. Varieties of heaths such as alpine bilberry and mountain cranberry survive doggedly in niches of scant earth.

Beyond the second lake, on rising ground, the Camel Trail branches right to Boott Spur, and the Tuckerman Crossover leads to Tuckerman Junction above the Ravine. Keep on the Crawford Path. It is well worn. It is marked by cairns, each topped with a yellow-painted rock. The gradual climb here is straight toward Washington's summit. The Davis Path joins from the right as you near the actual ascent of the cone. Not far beyond, the Westside Trail splits left to circle the cone for climbers heading toward the northern peaks of the Presidential Range—Clay, Jefferson, Adams, and Madison. Watch for this fork and be sure to bear right; although the cairn markers are the same, there's no chance of confusion in clear weather.

Mount Washington's summit beckons ½ mile ahead. You pass patches of tough Bigelow sedge, which thrives in this

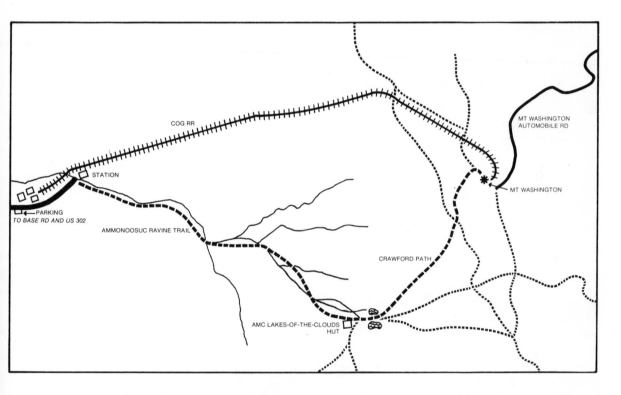

exposed situation. Juncos also appear at home. Now you go up the cone in a passage among rocks. You climb the final shoulder and look away to the northern peaks. The Gulfside Trail comes in left from these peaks. You approach the summit from the north up the last rock slope.

Your introduction to the modern age on the summit can be jarring—television towers and transmitter buildings, weather observatory, steam engines, sightseeing passengers, cars down in the parking area, the Summit House, and the old stone Tip-Top House. You approach these through the forgotten stone walls that once formed a corral for mountain ponies. You pass a popular viewpoint on your right, then the observatory. You come to the railway track and the Summit House. You are in the fifty-nine–acre Mount Washington State Park. The top of the world in northeastern America is a rock behind the Summit House, 6,288 feet above sea level.

The object of the climb to Mount Washington's Alpine Garden is enjoyment of the mountain rather than its conquest. This loop climb, with the Garden as its destination, is a treat. The alpine-arctic environment there affords more attractions than the tourist mecca on the summit. In 3 hours you climb from the temperate zone to an arctic waste.

Yet despite its barren appearance, this mile-high "garden" displays many of the 110 plant species that live above tree-line on Mount Washington and other Presidential peaks. Of this total, 75 are never found below these altitudes in New Hampshire. Most of the alpine plants occur at lower elevations in Alaska, northern Canada, Greenland, and arctic Eurasia.

The flower time, mid-June to July, brings to the Alpine Garden a miraculous shower of colors. Then you see yellow alpine avens, white diapensia, purple Lapland rosebay, and pink bilberry. The grasses, such as Bigelow sedge and

Alpine flowers

The Alpine Garden on Mount Washington

37. The Alpine Garden

Distance (round trip): 8½ miles.
Walking time: 6½ hours.
Vertical rise: 3,500 feet.

three-forked rush, sprout new green blades.

The Alpine Garden's plateau interrupts Mount Washington's steep eastern slope. A curving, mile-long shelf between Tuckerman Ravine and Huntington Ravine, the Garden begins and ends above these tremendous gorges. You look into dizzying depths and contrast them with the spaciousness of the sweeping views across Pinkham Notch to the Carter and Wildcat Ranges.

The climb to this elemental world begins at the AMC Pinkham Notch Camp 10 miles north of Jackson on NH 16. Park on the old road west of the present NH 16.

Walk past the lodge and turn right onto the Tuckerman Ravine Trail. (See hike number 32.) Follow this path for about 300 feet and watch on your right for the trail to the Old Jackson Road. It leads through open woods to a junction where the unused section of the Old Jackson Road comes in from the highway. This ancient woods road, now a trail, takes you in 1½ miles to the Mount Washington Automobile Road, about 2 miles

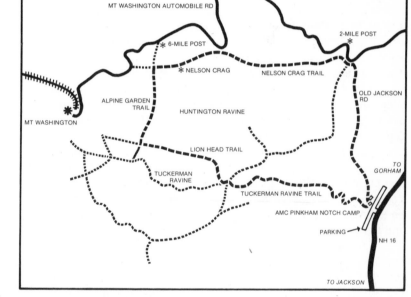

from NH 16. The auto road, completed in 1861, was actually built for horses and is still known as the Carriage Road. Keep up it a few yards to the left-branching trail to Nelson Crag. Don't take the nearby Raymond Path to Tuckerman Ravine.

The Nelson Crag Trail heads north away from the Raymond Path and almost at once goes

directly at the mountain. Another 1 mile takes you up to treeline and ledges and views of Pinkham Notch. Then for a short distance the trail joins the auto road before turning left into the rocks again. Up a steep ridge you climb to Nelson Crag. You are more than 1 mile above sea level.

Beyond Nelson Crag you come to the crossing of the Alpine

The Alpine Garden on Mount Washington

Garden Trail. (The Nelson Crag Trail continues between two rock-strewn knolls and joins the auto road again about 6½ miles up from NH 16.) At this junction take a good look at the weather. If you have any inkling that it will deteriorate in the next few hours or even if you are encountering ordinary clouds that are common above treeline, there is no point in continuing. The Alpine Garden is a gloomy rock field in cloud, and the cloud may be a warning of the deadly storms that blast Mount Washington. To retreat, turn right (north) on the Alpine Garden Trail and follow it to the auto road. Follow the auto road down to the Old Jackson Road for the return to Pinkham Notch Camp.

But, of course, if you've picked a clear day for this climb, the skies are blue and the sun is dazzling. In that happy event, turn left (south) from the Nelson Crag Trail onto the Alpine Garden Trail.

Soon you descend over rocks with views of Huntington Ravine on your left and the cone of Mount Washington on your right. A great cairn marks the junction with the Huntington Ravine Trail. Keep straight across. (The Huntington Ravine Trail climbs right ¼ mile to the auto road. To your left, it descends over the dangerous rocks in the Ravine.) Now you are in the Alpine Garden, and ahead stretches the mile of scattered, broken stones among which grow the dwarf spruces, alpine plants, and shrubs. A pause for lunch gives you time to look about and absorb both the desolation and the life on this plateau, where plants not only survive but blossom in colors to match the rainbow.

(Warning note: Don't pluck or disturb the plants; they're unique, and they're protected. Don't drink from the little brook that crosses the Alpine Garden; it's contaminated by drainage from the summit.)

As you proceed, keep to the Alpine Garden Trail. Follow the cairns. The trail's worn rocks and tracked soil will guide you if a cloud descends— but pay attention. You cross a broad flat as you approach Tuckerman Ravine and the intersection with the Lion Head Trail. (The Alpine Garden Trail continues another ¼ mile to the Tuckerman Ravine Trail.)

Turn left on the Lion Head Trail for the magnificent views along the rim of Tuckerman Ravine. In June you will probably gaze down at skiers on late snow in the Ravine. The trail leads you over Lion Head's granite brow and down steeply into the evergreen scrub and the lower spruce/fir woods. At the junction with the Tuckerman Ravine Trail, turn left. The trail is a tractor road here, which takes you down to Pinkham Notch Camp, 2¼ miles of easy walking.

The Alpine Garden on Mount Washington

38. Mount Jefferson

Distance (round trip): 6½ miles.
Walking time: 6 hours.
Vertical rise: 2,700 feet.

The sensational view south from Mount Jefferson's summit owes its fame to a vast glacial cirque, the Great Gulf, backed by the towering crags of Mount Washington. A remote peak of the Presidential Range if approached from the north, south, or east, and the third highest at 5,715 feet, Jefferson conceals its western access under the spruces that grow in Jefferson Notch. There the Caps Ridge Trail leaves the road and surmounts a sharp, west spur for the 2½-mile climb to the summit. Caps Ridge, however, should be approached warily rather than with the assurance that you've found the mountain's weak spot. The Caps Ridge Trail ascends the equivalent of a vertical ½ mile. There's no water.

The ledges, or Caps, challenge your legs and lungs. And the Caps present treacherous footing during or after a rainstorm.

From Mount Jefferson's summit, another spectacular shoulder, Castellated Ridge, provides a descent down the scenic Castle Trail, and a return route via the wooded Link Trail

back to Caps Ridge Trail and Jefferson Notch. About 3 miles of this 6½-mile loop are above treeline.

To reach Jefferson Notch, turn off US 302 at Fabyan and follow the road toward the cog railway's Base Station. Drive about 5 miles to an intersection. Turn left there onto the Jefferson Notch Road (gravel). Careful driving and occasional use of low gear take you 3 miles up to 3,000 feet. Park on the right. You are in Jefferson Notch.

The Caps Ridge Trail leads east through green spruce/fir woods. In less than ½ mile you pass the Link Trail on the left. (Take note of this junction. You'll return along the Link on the loop from the summit.)

The Caps Ridge Trail begins the real climb. Soon you catch glimpses of Mount Washington on the right. The view opens at a smooth ledge, right, in which small potholes indicate glacial action. You clamber up to treeline below the first of two rocky outcrops called the Caps. About ¼ mile above, as the ridge becomes a saw-

tooth edge, you climb the second Cap. You are exposed to all the mountains and sky. You're also exposed to the weather. If you see signs of rain, fog, or high winds, turn back while you can.

Climbing on under clear skies, you descend from the last Cap and start up the broad main peak. You cross the Cornice Trail, which for a few yards joins your Caps Ridge Trail. (The Cornice Trail, avoiding Jefferson's summit, offers a rough route left, north, to Edmands Col. To the right it swings southeast and joins the Gulfside Trail.) Here on the mountainside, open to the most violent and frigid winds, grass-like sedges and rushes thrive in little slanting meadows among acres of broken rock. These green swaths in the fall, August at this altitude, change to soft, pale tan colors.

Above the Cornice intersection, you may guess the next rise to be the summit, but you climb over two more before the cairns lead slightly left up the summit crags. Now you discover that Jefferson's summit consists of three crests bordering a lower flat, where signs mark the trail junction.

Each crest gives you an interesting perspective across the Great Gulf toward Mount Washington, its auto road, and summit buildings. The southeast ledges overlook Gulfside Trail's yellow-topped cairns crossing above the two ridges known as Jefferson's Knees. Looking east across Edmands Col to Mount Adams, you notice that it hides the last peak in the range, Mount Madison.

Your return loop begins at the junction between Jefferson's crests—in the hollow just east of the main summit—where you turn north onto Castle Trail. (If a storm breaks, you need a quicker escape route from these barren crests: follow the Jefferson Loop Trail instead. From the junction it leads northeastward toward Mount Adams. It will take you past Six Husbands Trail down to Gulfside Trail and Edmands Col, where you can take refuge in the emergency shelter. No camping.)

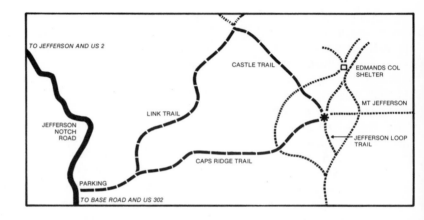

On Castle Trail cairns mark the way between the summit, left, and a rise of broken ledges, right. Swinging more northwest, you leave the small flat and descend toward distant rocks called the Castles. You follow a line of cairns easily spotted by their white quartz tops. The Castle Trail crosses the Cornice Trail. Less easily followed here, the cairns keep you seeking and picking your way down the scattered rock slabs toward the Castles. These vertical pinnacles overlook Castle Ravine's green depths. The trail becomes rougher and more difficult. It winds general ly below, but sometimes over, the western crags along the narrow ridge.

After the ledges beyond the largest Castle, you descend steeply below treeline. The intersection with the Link Trail comes 10 minutes later.

Turn left on the Link. (The Castle Trail continues down the ridge to Bowman on US 2.) For the first mile, the link crosses rough terrain over roots and rocks. Beyond a brook and during the second mile, the trail improves as it descends gradually through evergreen woods to Caps Ridge Trail. There, you turn right for Jefferson Notch and your car.

Mt. Jefferson

Mount Jefferson

Mount Jefferson

Mount Adams

39. Mount Adams

Distance (round trip): 9 miles.
Walking time: 7½ hours.
Vertical rise: 4,500 feet.

Mount Adams fascinates and challenges many hikers more than any peak in the Presidential Range. It offers deep ravines and long ridges. Majestic views across the Great Gulf toward Mount Washington greet you from the summit crags. Mounts Jefferson and Madison seem like neighbors. Second in height to Washington at 5,798 feet, Mount Adams when climbed from the north demands 231 more vertical feet than Mount Washington from Pinkham Notch. This ruggedness guarantees no tourists.

The shortest trail up Mount Adams begins at Appalachia, a former railroad flagstop that is now a parking space south of US 2. The Air Line Trail goes straight up prominent Durand Ridge.

Take US 2 west from Gorham's traffic lights. Drive 5½ miles over Gorham Hill and across Moose River. You identify Appalachia on the left (south) by the row of hikers' cars even before you see the signs "Trails Parking."

Mt. Adams, from Mt. Jefferson

Walk across the Boston and Maine tracks. For a few yards the route is jointly followed by Air Line and Valley Way Trails. (You will return by Valley Way.) The trails fork under the power line. Follow Air Line right. You enter maple woods. Various trails begin to branch from both sides of Air Line. You pass the Link and Amphibrach. Next, you pass the crossing of Sylvan Way, then later, Beechwood Way. Then Short Line branches right, and you cross Randolph Path, all in the first mile. Keep on Air Line.

The trail goes up soon enough. Expect an abrupt rise beyond a spring on your left off the trail. Better fill a canteen. The steep and uneven section of the trail takes you up Durand Ridge. You pass the junction of Scar Trail coming in on the left, then after ½ mile you pass Upper Bruin; both trails connect to Valley Way in the valley of Snyder Brook.

Durand Ridge, reaching above treeline, sharpens to the Knife-edge. You clamber past rocks that overlook the precipitous King Ravine on your right.

From the Ravine comes a trail, Chemin des Dames ("Ladies' Road"), which is the "easy" way up from that mysterious giant gorge named for its 1857 explorer, the Reverend Starr King. You look down upon rocks the size of houses. Hidden in caves under them, ice never melts. The Ravine, by legend, is the resting place for a starving band of Rogers's Rangers retreating after their retaliatory attack on the St. Francis Indian village in Canada during the French and Indian War.

Air Line next takes you past a branch trail, left, to AMC's Madison Hut, which is situated near the barren col between Mount Adams and Mount Madison. You keep on Air Line and climb steeply past the King Ravine Trail, right, at an entrance between ledges forming the Gateway into that glacial cirque.

Air Line joins the Gulfside Trail, coming in at the left, and they merge for a few yards. Mount Madison is in full view northeast.

Mount Adams

(If you're caught by one of the notable Mount Adams thunderstorms, which feature virtuoso lightning bolts, and your hair seems inclined to stand on end, turn left onto Gulfside Trail for a descent to shelter at Madison Hut. Yellow-painted stones top Gulfside cairns.)

The Air Line Trail soon forks left off the Gulfside Trail. (Gulfside continues around Mount Adams toward Mount Jefferson and Mount Washington.) Air Line climbs past a minor summit, on the left, named John Quincy Adams for the sixth president, and takes you up among rock slabs to the main peak of Mount Adams.

The summit spreads out before you a tremendous view into the Great Gulf. You feel as though you were leaning over the abyss, not because of sheer cliffs but because of the vastness. Mount Washington's superior height and size dominate the south outlook; the summit buildings are three and one-half miles away. Across the Gulf on a winding

ribbon up the slopes, small bugs, which are cars, creep along the auto road. At the horizon to your right, Mount Jefferson stands jagged against the sky; to your left, Mount Madison. Turning around northward, you see below you a lesser crest, named for the revolutionary of the Adams family—Sam Adams—and rising beyond is Thunderstorm Junction, where Gulfside Trail meets other trails at a huge cairn. In this north view on a clear day, you see the two bare Percy Peaks in the distance and the ridges near the Canadian border. More to the east, Umbagog Lake sparkles in the forest at the end of Maine's Rangeley Lakes chain.

For your descent, retrace your steps down Air Line as far as Gulfside Trail. Keep past the place where Air Line forks left and stay on Gulfside for the steep drop into evergreen scrub near Madison Hut. The Gulfside Trail ends at the Hut.

Take Valley Way Trail for your return to Appalachia. Valley Way descends rapidly into the Snyder Brook valley and offers protection from storms after

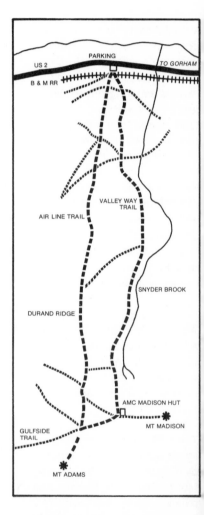

you enter the woods. Follow it past and across several trails, until it joins Air Line as you complete the loop and approach Appalachia.

40. Mount Madison

Distance (round trip): 10½ miles.
Walking time: 8 hours.
Vertical rise: 3,800 feet.

This rock pyramid completes the Presidential Range's northern peaks. Tourists and hikers alike see its bare crags towering above the northern approach to Pinkham Notch. Of its 5,363 feet, 4,500 rise directly from the Androscoggin River valley. It juts above teeline into the alpine-arctic environment of fragmented rock slabs, cold fogs, wind, and scanty vegetation. The peak is particularly impressive from NH 16 near the entrance to the Mount Washington Automobile Road, where the Osgood Trail begins. Hikers for almost a hundred years have enjoyed this scenic trail to Mount Madison's summit. From the auto road into the Great Gulf, the Osgood Trail bears north as a pleasant woods walk, which limbers early morning legs and relaxes them on the return at evening. On Osgood Ridge from treeline up, fine views extend south and west into the Great Gulf, across to Mount Washington, and along the range that sweeps over Mount Jefferson and Mount Adams to Madison. The route of this hike includes not only Osgood Ridge and Mount Madison's summit, but also AMC's Madison Hut and a return loop through Madison Gulf. The climb should be saved for a shining clear day.

Moonrise over Mt. Madison

Mount Madison

Turn west off NH 16 at the Mount Washington Automobile Road. Park in the area at the left (south) of the entrance. With your pack equipped for a climb into the arctic zone, walk across the auto bridge spanning Peabody River, pass the toll office, and follow the auto road across the field. At the woods, the Osgood Trail begins on your right.

The trail turns left uphill into spruces, then becomes a level pathway through the hardwoods. You enter an open area recently slashed by loggers, and the trail is muddy in places. Entering woods again, you cross a brook and descend gradually to a dry brook bed and the footbridge over a deep pool in the Peabody River's rushing West Branch. Cross the bridge. The trail bears left through moist woods for a few yards, then rises to the junction with the Great Gulf Trail from Dolly Copp Campground near NH 16.

Stay on the Osgood Trail. It crosses the Great Gulf Trail diagonally and continues up an easy grade among beech and yellow birch. You walk above the Great Gulf Trail for ¾ mile.

If you listen, you can hear the West Branch pouring over boulders and into pools.

Before the Osgood Trail takes you to serious climbing, it swings north along a small brook, where you should fill your canteen. The Madison Gulf Cutoff forks left. (Take notice, because you'll return by the Madison Gulf Cutoff.) Bear right on the Osgood Trail. You start climbing in earnest. At a big boulder on your right, you pass the Osgood Cutoff, left. Like the previous Madison Gulf Cutoff, it links up with the Madison Gulf Trail and thereby leads to Madison Hut via a less-exposed, steep, rough climb that avoids Madison's summit.

Stay on the main Osgood Trail. This steep section must be dealt with by the patience formula: one boot in front of the other. You climb through fine spruce woods. You're on a section of the Appalachian Trail, and are also following the boundary of the White Mountain National Forest's 5,552-acre Great Gulf Wilderness.

The spruces diminish in size; they become sparse and scattered. You look up from your climbing and find yourself in the wind and skies among rocks that rise ahead crest after crest.

Pause here and try to predict the weather. Fierce gales blast Osgood Ridge, and storms come up rapidly. It's a long, rugged, unsheltered mile over a series of high rock piles. You can easily turn back here.

Fair skies and breezes are the signal to continue to climb up the craggy peaks. Follow the cairns among the rock slabs and over the ledges. You are on the crest of Osgood Ridge, which curves left as well as up. You climb down a few yards over massive rocks to a narrow east-west flat. Trail signs mark this as Osgood Junction. The Daniel Webster Trail comes in on the right from Dolly Copp Campground. On the left, the Parapet Trail offers a 1-mile circuit below Madison's summit to Madison Hut. (Very acceptable in a sudden rain storm.)

The Osgood Trail goes up steeply again over the rocks along the ridge to Madison's northeast shoulder. It swings left down into a brief level section before the climb up the final pinnacle. On rising rocks again, you pass the Howker Ridge Trail, right. The Osgood Trail winds up westward among broken ledges.

At the summit, you stand on the big rocks that mark the end of the Presidential Range. The mountainside plunges northward into the valley. In that direction, the Watson Path drops off the summit. To the southeast you look down at your car parked near the auto road entrance. Clouds may come pouring out of the northwest before you have studied Mount Washington and the cars rounding the auto road's corner called the Horn, which you see across the Great Gulf. Mount Adams on the west often catches cloud wisps or disappears entirely.

The return route begins on the summit as part of a loop into Madison Gulf. Keep west on the Osgood Trail along

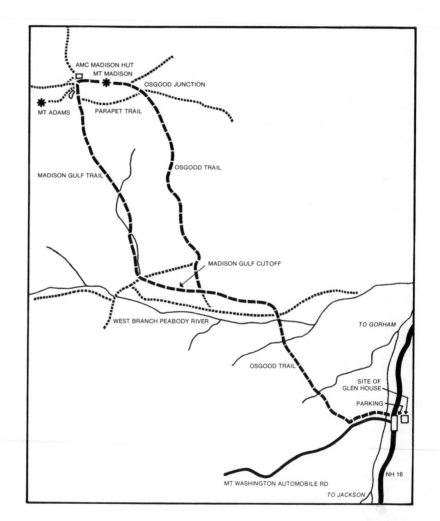

the jagged ridge beyond Madison's summit. The trail, marked by cairns, bears left off the ridge and descends the shoulder to Madison Hut below the looming crags of Mount Adams. The stone hut, where AMC hutmen provide meals and lodging for fifty hikers, serves also as a terminus for the Osgood Trail and various trails north and west.

Your route leaves the Hut, south, by the Parapet Trail. Climb up the slope and keep left at the branch trail to tiny Star Lake. Across the col, Parapet Trail makes a sharp left turn as you approach the look-off ledges. Then, it descends into a gully and the Madison Gulf Trail begins, right. (Parapet Trail keeps on toward Osgood Junction.) Turn right onto the Madison Gulf Trail. Climb down carefully over the steep, slippery rocks among scrub spruces.

The trail descends the Gulf by abrupt pitches between more gradual traverses, with many crossings of Parapet Brook. About 1½ hours from treeline, you make the last crossing over the brook's smooth rocks, to the east bank, and soon come to a trail junction. Your route, the Madison Gulf Cutoff, keeps straight ahead. (The Madison Gulf Trail turns down to the right. The Osgood Cutoff begins left up the bank.)

Walk ½ mile along the easy Madison Gulf Cutoff. You pass above the Great Gulf Shelter Number 3 and reach the junction seen early in the day at the Osgood Trail. Keep down the Osgood Trail on the now-familiar route across the Great Gulf Trail and over the West Branch footbridge for the walk back to the auto road and your car.

41. Mount Pequawket

Distance (round trip): 6 miles.
Walking time: 5 hours.
Vertical rise: 2,600 feet.

If you start climbing Mount Pequawket at dawn and if the day stays clear, you'll see the shining wet rocks of Tuckerman Ravine's headwall sixteen miles north on Mount Washington; to the right, Lion Head's cliff glows, and Huntington Ravine's rock facade catches sunlight in a bright chasm.

Official maps show the mountain as Kearsarge North, which distinguishes it from the Kearsarge near Warner. But Pequawket it was for forty-two years, and still is to many hikers. The Pequawket Indians hunted and raised corn in the Conway-Fryeburg forests and meadows along the Saco River.

Mount Pequawket became a popular summit for white men after 1845, when three enterprising men cut a bridle path to the 3,268-foot top and built a two-story wooden inn. The structure survived many years until an autumn gale blew it loose from its iron mooring rods and chains. Rebuilt, it stood for twenty-five more years before the winds blew it apart. A 1951-vintage fire tower now occupies the summit ledge, but, like others

View toward Mt. Pequawket

Mount Pequawket

in the mountains, it is no longer manned by a lone watcher; air patrols have taken over.

If you climb Mount Pequawket in the fall after snow has dusted the Presidentials, you'll understand the note on an eighteenth-century map issued during the French and Indian War, when this land was known only to hunters, trappers, and Indians. The note read "These WHITE HILLS appear many Leagues off at Sea like great bright Clouds above the Horizon, & are a noted Land Mark to Seamen."

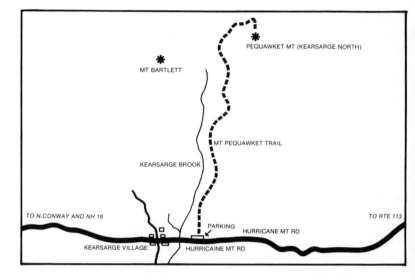

Drive about 2 miles north from North Conway on NH 16. Pass the scenic outlook to Mount Washington. Cross the railroad tracks and turn right onto the Hurricane Mountain Road. Drive through Kearsarge Village. Less than ½ mile beyond, the Mount Pequawket Trail starts on the left at a trail sign and small parking area.

The trail enters the woods and traverses tree-grown fields of the former Eastman farm; once a shady lane led to the house and barn. Steven Eastman built this lower trail through his pasture about 1872 as a link to the bridle path at Prospect Ledge. Now the farm has returned to forest.

The true ascent begins after the first ½ mile. Steadily upward the trail progresses through hardwoods of maple, beech, and birch to open rocks sparsely grown to sumacs and evergreens. You follow cairns and paint marks over slanting Prospect Ledge. There are wide views to the Saco valley south and west.

In the woods again and ½ mile farther, a good midway resting point, you come to a spring, down the bank to the right. (The summit is dry.) Climb on for another ½ hour along an ascending forest trail to more open ledges and scattered trees. Gradually you pass the minor wooded summit, Mount Bartlett, on your left and swing north and east around ledges again. Turning south for the final climb, you follow cairns and worn paths up the last rocks among spruces to the summit ledge and tower. You first look straight ahead to Maine and its lakes. Then you turn left, and the Presidential Range takes all your attention.

Mount Pequawket

42. Tom-Field-Avalon Loop

Distance (round trip): 8 miles.
Walking time: 6 hours.
Vertical rise: 2,800 feet.

Trails south from Crawford Notch link Mount Tom, Mount Field, and Mount Avalon for a loop hike. Spruces cloak Mount Field and Mount Tom, but both summits reach above 4,000 feet: Mount Tom, 4,047 feet, and Mount Field, 4,326 feet. Mount Avalon, a bare rock escarpment at 3,432 feet, overlooks Crawford Notch toward Webster Cliff and Mount Washington.

To begin the hike, drive to the Crawford House on US 302 at the western end of the Notch. Park north of the highway in an area designated by a Crawford Path sign. Walk across US 302 and proceed through the Crawford House grounds by the east path to the end of the building, which is near the footbridge over the railroad.

The Avalon Trail starts beyond this bridge. Your loop hike will take you up the Avalon Trail to the A-Z Trail and Mount Tom, then the Willey Range Trail to Mount Field, back down the Avalon Trail to Mount Avalon, and then back to the Crawford House.

A wide path entering the woods beyond the tracks, the Avalon Trail leads you past a trail to Mount Willard, left, which offers less-ambitious members of a party a spectacular view for only 1½ miles of upgrade. The Avalon Trail goes on to Beecher Cascade, where it crosses the brook and soon passes another trail, left, this one to Pearl Cascade.

You climb steadily for about 1 hour. The path becomes a mountain trail in spruce/fir woods. The A-Z Trail forks right. This is the beginning of the loop. Bear right onto the A-Z Trail. (You will return to this junction at the end of your hike.)

The A-Z Trail drops into and climbs out of a rough gully, then angles up for ½ mile to the last trickling brook. You begin the steep, rough ½-mile climb that takes you up to the height of land between Mount Tom and Mount Field.

A spur trail leads right for the ¾-mile climb to Mount Tom's summit. It winds through evergreens and across a short section of blown-down trees favored by juncos and white-throated sparrows. You swing around south to the summit, which you recognize by the sign on a tree and the end of the trail.

A quiet lunch among Mount Tom's spruces and firs may reveal dark spruce grouse feeding toward you among the ferns and wood sorrel or pecking at the evergreen needles. The male sports a red eyebrow. In sunlight and shade, his black and gray feathers hide him until he moves. This denizen of remote conifer forests is protected by New Hampshire law. His deliberate actions and lack of fear caused early hunters to think of domestic fowl and name him and his mate "fool hens."

After lunch, retrace your steps to the A-Z Trail and turn right. Follow it a short distance to the Willey Range Trail, which branches left toward Mount Field. (The A-Z Trail keeps on into the valley to the Zealand Trail and AMC's Zealand Falls Hut, more than 3 miles away.)

The Willey Range Trail leads up by easy grades through open growths of fir, spruce, and birch. Keep on past the junction

Tom-Field-Avalon Loop

where the Avalon Trail descends, left. You reach the summit of Mount Field in another 100 yards. As on Mount Tom, a sign marks the high ground in the woods. (The Willey Range Trail continues southeast over to Mount Willey and the Ethan Pond Trail.)

On Mount Field's summit, the trees open toward Crawford Notch and the peaks leading to Mount Washington. While you stand there admiring the outlook and settling your pack for the descent, don't be surprised if a hummingbird zooms over your head; if you have one of the bright new red or orange day-glo packs, it may appear to him like a patch of blossoms against the green trees.

Return to the Avalon Trail for the descent. It drops sharply down the side of Mount Field through low spruces. Care should be taken here: the footing on broken stones, wet turf, and occasional mud is often treacherous. The flat shoulder leading toward Mount Avalon's rocks provides blueberries in

Spruce grouse

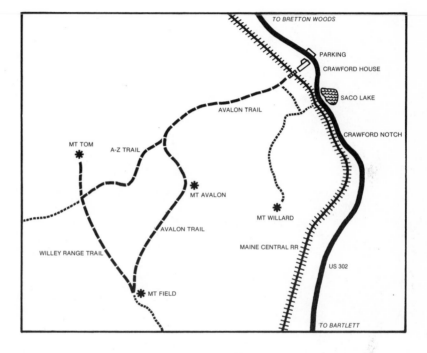

August along with views north and east.

The main trail bypasses the crest of Mount Avalon, but a side trail leads to the right a few yards up the rocks for a bird's-eye view of Crawford Notch and the white hotel 1,500 feet below. Don't miss this lookoff because you are a bit weary. You'll see the highway parallel to the railroad winding through the Notch; one of the great passes of the

Northeast. Webster Cliff is a stark mass of sheer rock buttressing the mountain northward. In the distance you gaze at the long Presidential Range centered on Washington's barren cone, which you identify by the buildings and broadcasting towers.

Below Mount Avalon, the trail continues to drop rapidly down through the spruces to the junction with the A-Z Trail, and the return to the Crawford House.

Tom-Field-Avalon Loop

43. Mount Starr King / Mount Waumbek

Distance (round trip): 7½ miles.
Walking time: 6 hours.
Vertical·rise: 2,600 feet.

A hiker in the White Mountains shuld see the Presidential Range from Mount Starr King. Thirteen miles northwest of Mount Washington across the upper valley of the Israel River, Starr King gives you a look at the complete panorama of the five rocky crests serrating the horizon eastward above the massed green slopes. From Mount Washington your eyes follow the skyline over Clay, Jefferson, Adams, and Madison.

In his 1859 book, the Reverend Thomas Starr King described the then-neglected views of the Presidentials from the north and northwest. He extolls Jefferson "Hill," which he says, "may without exaggeration be called the *ultima thule* of grandeur in the artist's pilgrimage among the New Hampshire mountains, for at no other point can he see the White Hills themselves in such array and force." The Reverend Mr. King gives no account of climbing summits north of present US 2, but his name is fittingly given to the

On Mt. Starr King

mountain that is the great lookoff for studying and enjoying the northern slopes of the Presidentials.

Drive to the Waumbek Hotel in Jefferson on US 2. Turn north off the highway across from the hotel entrance and follow a driveway leading uphill. Go left at a fork, then the next left. Drive carefully over water bars and past a concrete-walled sugar house. Bear right to park at the beginning of a bulldozed road.

The trail ascends straight up along an old logging road. You climb steadily through small hardwoods. Parallel on the left is the brook. You pass an old spring house on the right and then a pipe pouring out water from a big spring up on the bank. Keep to the right at the fork not far above the pipe. In less than ½ mile, the trail turns right off the logging road and takes you up the mountain at an equable grade for ¾ mile. Then it jogs right and left again at a boundary stake. As you climb into the zone of spruce and fir toward 3,000 feet, you pass two springs on the trail's left slope. One fulfills all the requirements for an ideal cold spring; it trickles from under a ledge into a shallow pool. The trail swings around to the north as it continues up and up. It approaches the summit from that direction.

Spruces screen partial views from the ledges near the big cairn there. Proceed along the trail about 200 feet through the trees. You abruptly emerge into the clearing, and there before you, peak after peak— the Presidentials! You scarcely notice on the left a closed-in log shelter and stone fireplace.

Sunlight alternates with cloud shadows over the mountains. Often, mists gather around the rugged peaks of Mounts Adams and Washington. Binoculars bring out the Madison Hut at the col between Madison and Adams. You look into the depths of King Ravine on Adams. Watch for the train on the cog railway climbing Washington. Below your vantage point is the green valley of Israel River and Jefferson Meadows. In the distance you see Cherry Mountain with its summit tower. The Franconia Range seems far away beyond numberless small-

er mountains and ridges, but Lafayette's blue-green silhouette assures you that you're looking at Franconia Notch's giant. Your gaze inevitably returns to the main attraction, the Presidential Range.

When you finally look more to your left nearby, you notice a ridge eastward, where spruces rise to a wooded summit 1 mile away: Mount Waumbek, seemingly of no consequence. But a trail in that direction leaves from the clearing at the southeast corner of the shelter. It winds through the evergreens below the ridge, then ascends. Although roughly laid out among stumps and tree trunks, it is well worn by hikers adding another 4,000-foot mountain for their records. Mount Waumbek is higher than Starr King—4,020 feet against 3,913.

Waumbek offers glimpses of the Presidentials through spruces at the end of a short trail past the summit sign on a tree. Clouds whirl turbulently overhead and gather around Mounts Adams and Madison. The appeal of Waumbek is primitive, a north-

country wildness occasionally animated by small birds in the spruces—boreal chickadees and golden-crowned kinglets.

Return to the clearing on Starr King for a final scanning of the panorama before you, then descend through woods brightened by the lowering sun along the trail you climbed when the day was new.

Mount Starr King and Mount Waumbek

44. Mount Eisenhower

Distance (round trip): 6½ miles.
Walking time: 5 hours.
Vertical rise: 2,725 feet.

Southwest from Mount Washington, rocky peaks extend toward Crawford Notch. One of these, Mount Eisenhower (formerly Mount Pleasant), commands a spectacular view to all points of the compass.

This broad dome overlooks sections of the famous 8-mile Crawford Path from Crawford Notch. Three beeline miles to the north, past Mount Franklin's long hump and Mount Monroe's two crests, Washington pursues its role as the highest point in the Northeast: it hosts tourists carried to the top by cog railway and automobile; it supports the summit buildings, towers, and observatory; it tolerates—with occasional good weather—the many hikers on its exposed slopes.

Into the arctic-alpine world of Mount Eisenhower, the Edmands Path climbs up a west ridge and around the north base of the dome to the Crawford Path. There, near this junction, a side trail leads up the crags and over the rounded 4,761-foot summit. On a clear day, from that vantage point high above the forests, the sky and rocks are elemental and clean.

To reach the Edmands Path, turn off US 302 at Fabyan onto the Base Road leading to the cog railway's Base Station. Soon Mount Eisenhower comes into sight as a hemispherical outline contrasting with its more jagged neighbors and topped by a tiny spike pricking the skyline—actually a great cairn on the summit. Drive on the Base Road about 5 miles to an intersection. Turn right. You are

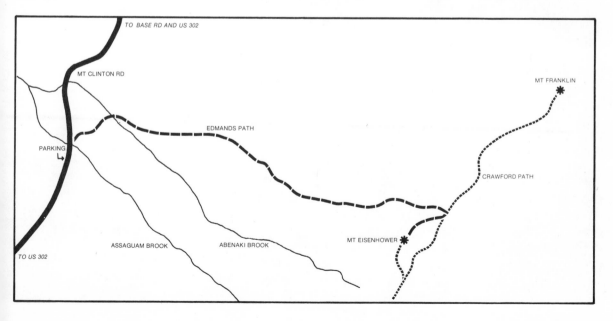

Mount Eisenhower

Mount Eisenhower

now on the Mount Clinton Road. Drive 1½ miles from the four corners. And drive carefully; there's a startling 90-degree curve about ½ mile from the trail.

The Edmands Path enters the woods on the left, east, just north of the culvert over Assaguam Brook. The great trail builder, J. Rayner Edmands, relocated and graded the path in 1909. It bears left through open woods among beech and yellow birch. It crosses a footbridge over Abenaki Brook. Keep to the right up an old logging road beside the brook. You begin to climb somewhat here. Then the trail swings left up the ridge that will take you to treeline. The grade steepens but is nowhere excessive. You enter spruce/fir woods, the habitat of the blackpoll warbler and Bicknells's thrush.

You climb up sections of graded fill held on the slope by rockwork. You notice rocks drilled and split with hand tools to clear and ease the way. Approaching treeline among small birches and spruces, you find the trail paved with flat stones. These are almost unbelievable monuments to Edmands's meticulous trail construction.

If a cloud thick as sea fog masks the rocks, or if a storm threatens, heed the Forest Service warning sign in the last trees, and turn back.

Once above treeline, you will see that the Edmands Path splits into three gravel trails between ledges and across alpine sward. Keep straight ahead up to the junction with the Crawford Path. Then turn right, south. After a few yards bear right again. This is the side trail over Mount Eisenhower whose rough dome rises ahead. (The Crawford Path bears left around the base.) You descend slightly and pass a little pool, Red Pond, on your left. Up the ragged ledges the trail zigzags, then takes you in a more gradual swing to the wide summit and the great cairn. The green cushions all across the summit are the alpine plant, diapensia. If you climb in mid-June, you'll see the array of white blossoms.

Walk around for the views. To the north, up Mount Franklin curves the old and honored Crawford Path, in use for 150 years. Dropping away east of Mount Franklin, the ledges disappear into Oakes Gulf, where the Dry River (Mount Washington River) begins its turbulent run to the Saco River. Beyond Mount Franklin, you see a small peak on the left and a higher crest right, which combine to form Mount Monroe. Then comes Washington, often crowned by a misty cloud.

Your return follows the same route to the Edmands Path junction with the Crawford Path. Turn left down to the graded way and into the trees. The construction so carefully carried out by J. Rayner Edmands makes the descent as nearly painless as your tired legs will experience anywhere. But this ease may trick you: it's likely to lull you so that the descent seems longer than the climb.

Mount Eisenhower

Mount Crawford

45. Mount Crawford

Distance (round trip): 5 miles.
Walking time: 4½ hours.
Vertical rise: 2,100 feet.

A rough oval of ledges around spruce scrub, Mount Crawford's 3,129-foot promontory extends into the broad delta of ridges and valleys that flow ten miles south from Mount Washington. Two great cliffs, 1½ miles northeast, the Giant Stairs, identify Stairs Mountain and the long, forested Montalban Ridge. The Presidential Range's southern peaks appear at the far north end of the Dry River valley. To the northwest, Mount Willey looms over Crawford Notch.

A former bridle path, cut fifteen years before the Civil War, passes east of Mount Crawford to Mount Washington. (A spur path rises to Mount Crawford's summit.) This route, called the Davis Path, was constructed by Nathaniel Davis, proprietor of the Mount Crawford House, and brother-in-law of the famous Ethan Allen Crawford. (The vanished Mount Crawford House should not be confused with the Crawford House now at the gateway of the Notch.) Nathaniel Davis sold his

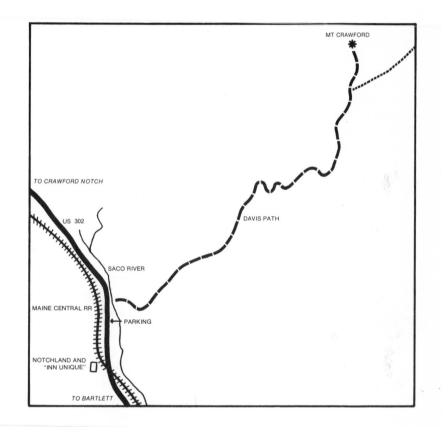

Near Mt. Crawford

horses about the time adventurous sightseers began riding up the Carriage Road being built from the Glen House in Pinkham Notch. After 1855 the bridle path fell into disuse and grew back to woods. In 1910, the AMC and volunteers reopened it, discovering, with the aid of a Maine woodsman, all the original path.

To make this historic and rewarding hike, drive about 6 miles west from Bartlett on US 302. Watch for a stone house, "The Inn Unique," on the left before a railroad crossing. You are at Notchland, which was once a station named Bemis, for the builder of the stone house. Drive across the railroad tracks a short distance to parking on the right. The Davis Path begins at the highway about 200 yards farther north.

The trail takes you over the shallow Saco River on a suspension footbridge. Cross an old field grown to bushes, passing a new house on your right, and step over a muddy brook channel. You climb slightly, then turn right and go along woods to a logging road into which the trail jogs sharply left. You walk through open woods and across a dry brook bed lined with smooth stones. The trail bears left, and you begin the climb along the old bridle path up the side of the ridge. The steady grade for a short distance parallels a brook on your left. This is the last water. As you keep going up more steeply on straight stretches dug from the slope, you walk along a section of trail where Nathaniel Davis built a rock retaining wall. You wonder at the strong backs and patience of the men who worked with oxen, chains, and crowbars. The graded trail reminds you of the untold miles of New England's stone walls.

You follow winding turns as you approach the top of the ridge. You emerge from spruces on open ledges, where you look northwest to Crawford Notch and Mount Willey. Keep right, over two wave-like swells and across an arm of spruce woods to rock again. Watch for cairns ahead and white paint marks on the ledges among scattered spruces.

You come to a long slanting rock face. The Davis Path turns right. The spur trail to Mount Crawford's summit goes up across the rock face.

At the top, the path continues among ledges and spruces, marked by a few cairns. The paint blazes on the rocks have faded, but the trail stays on the ridge crest, and about ¼ mile from the Davis Path you step out on the cliff that looks off to the Giant Stairs and the gravel slides on Montalban Ridge. Ledges continue around a small growth of spruces, with views up Dry River— misnamed because it can be a turbulent, dangerous stream— to Mount Eisenhower, Mount Franklin, Mount Monroe, and

Mount Washington. Walk around and look southwest to Mount Carrigain and its tower. To your left, down in the valley, you see the stone house and the highway. Mount Crawford gives you a complete 360-degree panorama for your 2½-mile climb.

Giddy from mountain vistas, you may for a change turn to the tiny cranberry vines clinging to rock crevices along with alpine crowberry. Labrador tea and blueberries grow in the shelter of the five-foot spruces. White-throated sparrows flit nearby. Cedar waxwings perch on dead twigs and survey the scene in their alert way. This is a place to linger, to look about again, and to eat a hearty lunch.

Mount Crawford

Backpacking Hikes

46. Mount Hancock

Time allowed: 2 days, 1 night.
Distance (round trip): 9½ miles.
Walking time (with pack for 5½ miles): 7½ hours.
Vertical rise (including both peaks): 2,400 feet.

Your first overnight hike should test, but *gently*. It should give you the chance to try out new boots, pack, tent, cooking kit, and food—and, most important, your own capacity. But it should not include too many miles, blistered feet, and exhaustion in the late afternoon when the time has come to cope with a strange sleeping arrangement and unaccustomed cooking methods. You want challenge, but not too much; you want new scenes and adventure. The trip to Mount Hancock meets these specifications.

The first day's hike to the base of the mountain is easy. The climb next day requires only sandwiches, water, and strong legs. (Or don't climb at all; loaf around camp and enjoy the woods and the brook. Those who want to climb can challenge the loop over the mountain's north and south summits.) Later that day you pack up and hike back to the highway.

The Hancock Notch Trail goes north from the Kancamagus Highway at the hairpin turn about 10½ miles east of Lin-

A backpaker's view of Mount Madison and Mount Adams

coln. Off the upper half of the hairpin is a parking area.

The trail follows a logging railroad grade through young hardwoods merging with spruce and fir as you swing east above Hancock Branch's North Fork. The grade curves around the west shoulder of Mount Huntington at about the 2,300-foot contour. In places, swampy ground nurtures lush sphagnum moss at either side of the packed fill. The rails have been gone since before World War I. Rows of blasted rocks still hold the fill in place. Cuts through ledge and banks are ten and twelve feet deep. The fast, easy walking is interrupted at gullies and brooks once spanned by log bridges.

The hurricane of September 1938 laid down the trees that had begun to reforest the cut-over ridges and valleys. At the same time, Mount Hancock's north and east slopes were logged clear of all merchantable trees. For many years thereafter, the Forest Service closed off and kept watch over the area until the forest fire danger passed and new growth healed the devas-

tation. The present trees demonstrate the rapid gains they make when protected.

About 1¾ miles in from the Kancamagus Highway, the Cedar Brook Trail branches left, northward, among spruce and fir. (The Hancock Notch Trail continues east to the height of land and down to Sawyer River, which drains into the Saco River south of Crawford Notch.)

Turn left onto the Cedar Brook Trail. The name derives from the brook on the far side of Mount Hitchcock, which is ahead and to your left, west of north. Mount Hancock is ahead and to the right, hidden like Hitchcock by trees. You are still following Hancock Branch's North Fork. You cross it five times in the next ¾ mile.

The brook takes on a rusty color. An old beaver pond, peat bogs, spruces, and tamaracks give the tan shade to the water. You follow the trail through a mossy bog where pitcher plants—those strange insect-eaters—grow near heavy turf interlaced with rootlets. The old logging road is wide, the bog in places is surfaced with

Mount Hancock

a corduroy of slippery logs.

Beyond the fifth brook crossing, watch on the right for the Hancock Loop Trail. It cuts into thicker woods from the more open area and crosses the brook to a good, although unofficial, campsite. You have carried your pack about 2¾ miles—far enough to have learned some packing tricks and trials, far enough to have felt, at least briefly, the exhilaration of carrying your home with you, the freedom of the backpacker.

The light nylon tent goes up quickly. Or it does if you've practiced in your back yard or even in your living room. Fluff out the down-filled sleeping bag. The traditional campfire may wait until you have cooked your freeze-dried meal on a backpacker's gasoline stove. Then a fire warms and cheers as darkness approaches. It may also attract white-footed mice hopping delicately near. Later, when you're dropping off to sleep, they will rustle in the pack's food bags if you left them on the ground, and you will have to wriggle out of

Backpacking near Mt. Hancock

Mount Hancock

your bag to hang the pack in a tree by flashlight, bare feet cold in the dew.

Next morning after breakfast, arrange sandwiches, raisins, candy bar, canteen, compass, and jacket—not forgetting the fly dope if it's early summer— and prepare for the trail, booted and ambitious. Perhaps you avoid overloaded pockets and belt-dangled equipment by shouldering a little waterproof nylon pack that can fold to envelope size when not needed for a day's excursion.

Beyond your camp, Hancock Loop Trail becomes rough in a steep, dry brook, then goes along the side hill at a moderate grade. There are sections, however, where dark muck traps your feet unless you bushwhack around. Beyond the young hardwoods and scattered evergreens, you catch glimpses of the slide identifying Mount Hancock's south slope. It's a slippery looking ledge appearing as smooth as gray glass above a jumble of rocks and gravel. Until recently, the climb was made up the slide.

Approaching the mountain, the trail, along an old logging

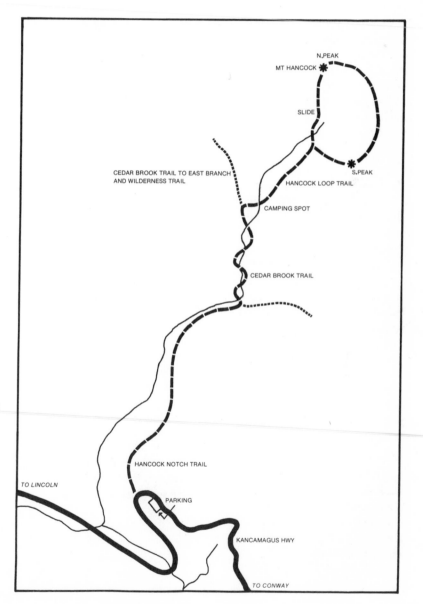

Mount Hancock

road, keeps above the brook, which begins at the base of the slide, where it's usually dry in summer. The trail junction for the loop over Mount Hancock's two summits overlooks the gully separating you from the slide on your left.

Both summits are more than 4,000 feet high, yet wooded. To climb the 4,403-foot north peak first—although the order chosen matters little—turn left down into the dry brook gully. The trail bears right, away from the slide's base, and enters the spruces. You climb up very steeply, but avoid the slide as the trail is cut up through the woods. Despite the angle, much larger spruces once grew here. You rest at monster stubs and fallen trunks, some charred from forest fire. One stub, three feet through at the butt, towers above the new growth.

From the north peak, which you reach at an opening in the short spruces near a summit sign, you have a slight view toward Mounts Lafayette and Garfield. To the east along the loop trail less than 100 yards, a spur trail leads off right to "Plymouth Rock" (which resembles the original). You gain a striking view to Mounts Washington and Carrigain.

From the north peak summit, the trail continues around eastward, descending the ridge, a narrow winding traverse up and down, around blowdowns, and across surprising wet spots. The trail gradually ascends the south peak to 4,274 elevation. An opening a few yards east gives you an outlook over the Sawyer River valley.

Beyond the south peak, the trail turns right, west, and drops sharply away down through spruce/fir woods to the end of the logging road that returns you to the junction where you began the loop. Of the total distance around the loop, 2¼ miles, all but the ridge mile has been up or down as steeply as almost any trail in the mountains, which explains the 3 hours it requires.

Retracing your earlier steps to camp, you have time for another meal before folding the tent and packing to hike out. For the return trip, 1½ hours should be enough time—less if you stride down the railroad grade like a veteran backpacker.

47. Sandwich Mountain

Time allowed: 2 days, 1 night.
Distance: 13 miles.
Walking time: 9½ hours.
Vertical rise: 2,500 feet.

Lunch on Sandwich Mountain

Viewed from a distance, the heavy silhouette that terminates the Sandwich Range's western reach contrasts with the much-photographed eastern pinnacle, Mount Chocorua. Sandwich Mountain rises massively from a broad foundation buttressed by ridges extending from Waterville Valley south to Beebe River and east to Flat Mountain Ponds. On the west, it slopes to Black Mountain above Sandwich Notch.

Sandwich Mountain appeals because it's a familiar, yet distant, landmark. Often seen from highways and from other summits, the mountain is less frequently climbed. Spruce/fir woods grow to the 3,993-foot summit, but ledges offer partial outlooks. On this hike, the climb up Black Mountain from the west provides the spectacular views lacking on Sandwich Mountain.

This is a loop hike with a long spur. Starting from the Sandwich Notch Road, you follow the Algonquin Trail to Black Mountain's bare ridge. There you leave your pack and con-

Sandwich Mountain

tinue on the Algonquin Trail to Sandwich Mountain, then return to Black Mountain. For the night's camp, you pack down to Black Mountain Pond Shelter. On the second day, woods trails take you back to the Sandwich Notch Road.

First Day

Sandwich Notch Road to Sandwich Mountain to Black Mountain Pond Shelter

Distance: 7½ miles.
Walking time: 6 hours.

This big day of the trip includes all your climbing. At least 6 hours should be allowed for the engaging 7½ miles.

From Campton, drive east on the Waterville Valley Road (NH 49) about 3½ miles to a right turn, south, onto the Sandwich Notch Road. Follow this narrow, steep, dirt road 3¾ miles to the Algonquin Trail, which begins on the left (northeast) side as a logging road. There is no designated parking here. Pull off the road and shoulder your pack.

The Algonquin Trail follows the logging road almost 1 mile, then branches left up toward the south face of Black Mountain. Climbing steadily, you come to the first ledges that will make this climb distinctive and open, but not difficult. Beyond a small brook, you climb again and reach the upper ridge, where the trail turns right on the bare shoulder leading to the summit.

The wide views include the nearby Sandwich Notch area. The Sandwich Notch Road has been in use from the early days of settlement and once was bordered by farms and houses. Conservationists, led by the Society for the Protection of New Hampshire Forests, have launched a campaign to save this territory from private exploitation.

The Algonquin Trail continues along the open ridge to a junction, at right, with the Black Mountain Pond Trail. The shelter on the pond is your destination for the night. Since you will return to this junction, you'll want to cache your pack here, taking along in one of those neat little

nylon packs a canteen, lunch, and jacket. From this junction you have a 1¾-mile spur that will take you over Black Mountain and up Sandwich Mountain.

Continue east on the Algonquin Trail. It crosses a ledge from which you look down at Black Mountain Pond 1,000 feet below. Swinging somewhat left and entering spruces, you climb to Black Mountain's summit. Watching the trail, and startled by droppings apparently left by a pony herd, you may not at first realize you're walking through a moose "yard." So dense are the spruce and fir trees that the moose find winter quarters under the protecting branches and food from the evergreen tips. Winter at 3,460 feet suits New Hampshire moose. Snow, crusting upper boughs, roofs a sheltered stable for the huge animals.

The Algonquin Trail now descends to the ridge that leads to Sandwich Mountain. You pass occasional ledges and outlooks north, but mostly you ascend through spruce/fir woods. The Algonquin Trail joins the Sandwich Mountain Trail for the last few yards to the summit. (The Sandwich Mountain Trail comes in, left, from the Waterville Valley Road.) The spruces hide much of the view, but from rocks near the large summit cairn you get a lookout over Waterville Valley to Mount Tecumseh's ski slopes and Mount Osceola's tower.

Retrace your route via the Algonquin Trail to the junction with the Black Mountain Pond Trail and your pack. Turn left (south) for the descent to the pond and shelter. The way is steep. Watch your footing and dig your heels in when gravity begins to get the best of you. The ledges and evergreens seem about to slide into the valley, yet they will probably stay in place. The tops of lower trees are on your eye level; you may have a close introduction to tiny golden-crowned kinglets. Approaching the base of this precipitous mountainside you descend through spruce woods that have never been cut. The trail levels out at beaver dams on the inlet to Black Mountain Pond. At the pond, the trail

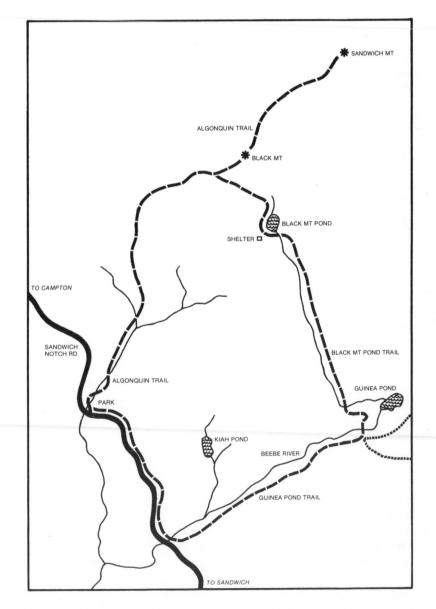

Sandwich Mountain

swings around the west shore, where you come to the open-front log shelter for eight hikers. The six-acre pond is thirty-two feet deep, clear, and the home of speckled trout.

Second Day

Black Mountain Pond Shelter to Sandwich Notch Road

Distance: 5½ miles.
Walking time: 3½ hours.

Easy walking this day leaves you free to swim and lie in the sun all morning. The pond is a gathering spot for birds and animals. Kingfishers, herons, cedar waxwings, blackbirds, and ducks enliven the shoreline. In the spruces, white-throated sparrows flit about, and red squirrels scold. At dusk or dawn, moose, white-tailed deer, and black bear come to the water. Mink and beaver appear almost anytime, and at night coons splash about in shallow water chasing frogs. (Not that you'll necessarily see all these, but you might.) From the shelter you look back up the steep slope you came down, and feel

pleased that you don't have to climb it.

After lunch, pack shouldered once more, you leave the shelter and follow the Black Mountain Pond Trail above the south shore. The trail descends, crosses the outlet brook below rocks, turns right, and keeps to the east bank of the brook on a downhill slant along an old logging road. After about 1½ miles, you cross to the west bank and continue along this woods trail to Beebe River, which is a brook here. On the far side, after a short distance, the Black Mountain Pond Trail ends at the Guinea Pond Trail. Turn right on the Guinea Pond Trail for the Sandwich Notch Road. (The Guinea Pond Trail to the left, east, connects with Flat Mountain Pond Trail and Bennett Street north of Whiteface Intervale, Sandwich. The Mead Trail, also at this junction, leads south up Mount Israel.)

The Guinea Pond Trail takes you west along a combined trail and jeep road through low ground and over ledges to a beaver pond and meadow

at a former logging railroad grade. This grade continues south of Beebe River past a power line. You leave the grade to dip down to the Sandwich Notch Road. Turn right (north) over the bridge across Beebe River. Follow the dirt road north about 1½ miles to the beginning of the Algonquin Trail and your car.

48. East Branch Region/Mount Carrigain

Time allowed: 3 days, 2 nights.
Distance (round trip): 28 miles.
Walking time: 21 hours.
Vertical rise: 3,300 feet.

A three-day weekend is ideal for this hike. You exchange your daily routine in the modern world for life in the remote Pemigewasset "Wilderness" between Crawford Notch and the Franconia Range. The pleasures of distant woods and high mountains, as well as the satisfaction of backpacking nearly 30 miles in three days, may escape you unless you've walked enough to toughen your legs. On the morning after the first day's 7-mile hike through Carrigain Notch, you'll want to rise from your sleeping bag eager for 13 miles exploring the trails to Shoal Pond and Thoreau Falls. And you'll really enjoy the trip if your legs still have plenty of spring in them for the third day's climb up 4,680-foot Mount Carrigain.

For each of the three days, there are unique experiences to anticipate. First, Carrigain Notch, a true hikers' pass between mountain and cliff, opens to the headwaters of the Pemigewasset River's East Branch, where you camp at Desolation Shelter. Second, in those secluded valleys you find miles of first-class walking because old logging railroads provide easy grades beside clear streams. Third, Mount Carrigain's summit surprises you as a triangulation point for the great ranges, and the splendid panorama draws all the mountains together into a coherent pattern.

Mount Carrigain's tower on the third day is the hike's culmination before you descend to your car and to civilization.

First Day

Carrigain Notch and
Desolation Shelter

Distance: 7 miles.
Walking time: 6 hours.

You start your trip with a walk into the wilds through Carrigain Notch. Drive west about 4 miles from Bartlett on US 302. Cross the bridge over Sawyer River and turn left onto the Sawyer River Road. On the right, 2 miles in, a small parking place accommodates cars at the start of the Signal Ridge Trail, which serves as a way to the Carrigain Notch Trail.

Shouldering your pack, you climb up Signal Ridge Trail by a logging road across Whiteface Brook, which pours through its little valley on your right as you climb the first ridge. The trail swings west away from the stream, and you enter a logged area. Avoid the side roads. After 1 hour or so from the car, you approach Carrigain Brook. The Carrigain Notch Trail forks right. Signal Ridge Trail bears left. Turn right onto Carrigain Notch Trail. (On the third afternoon, you'll descend Signal Ridge Trail from Mount Carrigain's summit to this junction.)

Now you head north along the Carrigain Notch Trail. It curves around Mount Carrigain, which is on your left but out of sight behind ridges and above the hardwood forest through which you walk. The trail follows Carrigain Brook by easy grades. As you near the stream's source below Carrigain Notch, you come to beaver dams and ponds that may obscure the way. Look ahead and to the right; you'll see the Notch's cliffs. The trail's short climb to the pass is plain enough after you leave Carrigain Brook.

Wild and unknown to many travelers, Carrigain Notch forms a gateway to the East Branch valley. On your left, a towering shoulder, Vose Spur, separates you from Mount Carrigain's main bulk. On the right, Mount Lowell rises above the cliffs that complete the gunsight formation of the Notch. The trail crosses beneath these heights among rocks and young spruces.

Still on the Carrigain Notch Trail, you are following an old logging road in more open country along boggy slopes west of Notch Brook. Your westerly direction takes you north of Mount Carrigain. Among small poplars and wild cherry trees, the trail meets a former railroad grade and turns sharply left. Nancy Pond Trail joins from the right. (The Nancy Pond Trail comes from Crawford Notch and US 302 at Notchland.)

Walking a wooded mile on the grade brings you to the site of vanished Camp 20 and a trail junction. The Carrigain Notch Trail turns abruptly right,

The East Branch of the Pemigewasset

East Branch Region and Mount Carrigain

downhill. The Desolation Trail leaves on the left; its name refers to the devastation once caused by logging. (From this junction on the third day, you'll climb Desolation Trail to Mount Carrigain's summit.)

Your first day's hike is almost complete, and you may rest or explore here at old Camp 20. It's typical of many deserted East Branch logging sites that have returned to woods. Built by J. E. Henry and Sons Company of Lincoln, this Camp 20 remains only as rotted boards grown over by raspberry bushes. A dump hidden under forest duff contains rusty tin cans, old peavey ferrules, sled runners, and pieces of cast iron stoves. Once the clearing was alive with hustling men and horses working in the woods from daylight until dark. Trains carried away the logs. Now, most hikers scarcely pause in walking by.

One hiker did. He tells of discovering evidence of toil and poverty. Near the dump he unearthed a rotted leather boot that had been resoled four times. Nails held leather to leather on this relic, and attested to a lumberjack's "making do" his only pair of boots. Yet the hiker recalled that many old lumberjacks look back upon their younger days in the camps and forests as the best years of their lives. (Rough on the forests, however.)

Turn right at Camp 20 as the Carrigain Notch Trail heads toward Desolation Shelter ¼ mile away where you will spend the night. Situated among spruces, which provided its three log walls, the shelter opens toward a boulder-strewn brook of transparent water—Carrigain Branch. The shelter sleeps eight hikers, and often attracts more than you'd guess from its remote location. When the shelter is occupied, a tent can be pitched nearby.

Second Day

Loop to Stillwater Junction, Shoal Pond, Thoreau Falls, East Branch, and back to Stillwater Junction

Distance: 13 miles.
Walking time: 8 hours.

This 13-mile walk along railroad grades and old haul roads benefits from an early start, which lengthens the day. Besides, as the sun begins to rise, you walk along the trail through cool woods; leaves and grass shine with dew, and the birds are singing.

From Desolation Shelter the Carrigain Notch Trail goes ½ mile down to its end at Stillwater Junction. There, three headwater streams merge to form the East Branch. Three trails join also: the Carrigain Notch Trail, Wilderness Trail, and Shoal Pond Trail. The junction once brought together the easternmost spur tracks of J. E. Henry's logging railroad.

The water is indeed still at Stillwater Junction—or, for a mountain stream, very nearly so. Gravel flats carry the slow

East Branch Region and Mount Carrigain

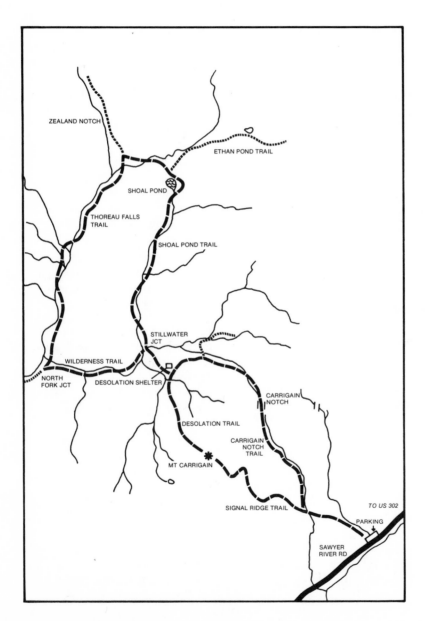

water to polished ledges, and the small river then sluices to its wide-open, stony bed for the nine-mile descent beside the Wilderness Trail to the Kancamagus Highway.

You will return to Stillwater Junction for your second night's camp after the day's loop hike. So you may elect to cache your pack in a tree, and take with you only lunch and equipment for a long hike. But if you leave your pack behind, you also leave behind your backpacker's freedom. You might want to keep open the possibility of camping at Thoreau Falls or elsewhere along the way. (If you camp at Thoreau Falls, there'll be an additional 7 miles the third day, but 7 miles less this day.)

From spruce/fir woods at Stillwater Junction, you take the north route, Shoal Pond Trail, across the footbridge over the East Branch. The trail soon lines out along the old railroad grade, straight for ½ mile through the new, young forest of poplar, wild cherry, white birch, and maple. You come to the first crossing of Shoal Pond Brook, which is

East Branch Region and Mount Carrigain

one of several in the 4 miles to Shoal Pond.

During logging days before World War I, standard-gauge steam locomotives chugged along the steel rails and cross-ties, that were later taken up, rotted, or burned. The stocky, tough little locomotives towed flatcars from Lincoln with men and supplies for the camps, and, when necessary as the trees were cut back, moved the camps themselves. The trains also carried Sunday excursionists, for a fee, and trout fishermen. The work trains returned to Lincoln piled high with spruce logs from landings along East Branch and such tributaries as Shoal Pond Brook.

The Shoal Pond Trail takes advantage of one of these landings near the site of Camp 21. These platforms stored logs for the trains and were manned by a gang of men wielding peaveys. A cribbing of tree trunks supported J. E. Henry's landings against a slope above the railroad. The cribbing held the level rollway above the tracks where the flatcars waited. Horse teams dragged the sled

loads from the haul roads to the landing and rested while peavey men rolled the logs off. Then the teamsters drove their horses back to the cutting woods. As many as 10,000 board feet of logs could be stored and rolled onto the flatcars below the landing. On the downgrade to the Lincoln sawmills, the flatcars shoved against the little engine. Brakemen scrambled over the slippery logs to primitive handbrakes. Link-and-pin couplings rattled, wheels clacked on rail joints, the engine chugged and thumped as it held back and blew out clouds of steam and smoke as well as sparks that often set the woods afire.

The scene now is quiet and verdant. The Shoal Pond Trail leads through part of the 18,560-acre Lincoln Woods Scenic Area set aside by the Forest Service in 1969 to remain safe from axe, saw, and bulldozer.

A young forest grows on the earth scorched by logging and fire. You walk in the shade of innumerable trees. Under National Forest protection since the early 1930s, this East Branch country has made a

miraculous recovery. The wonder of returning forest speaks loud and clear for conservation, yet might suggest to the thoughtful hiker that earth and nature have given man more reprieves than he deserves.

As you approach Shoal Pond, the trail crosses to the east bank of the brook. Beavers have taken over the pond's four acres, making themselves at home in water four feet deep at most. The trail has been relocated to avoid flooded woods and gnawed-down trees. A few hundred yards beyond the pond, the trail splits. Both forks lead to the Ethan Pond Trail. Take the left fork, which follows the old Zealand Notch railroad grade. This was another J. E. Henry enterprise that ended with fierce fires in 1886. Burned to bedrock, Whitewall Mountain north of you stands as testimony to the blazing inferno.

About ¾ mile from Shoal Pond, you reach the Ethan Pond Trail, where the Shoal Pond Trail ends. Keep left onto the Ethan Pond Trail.

For the purpose of this hike, the Ethan Pond Trail provides a ½-mile transfer to the Thoreau Falls Trail. (The Ethan Pond Trail comes from US 302 in Crawford Notch.) You follow the Ethan Pond Trail along the railroad grade to a crossing of the East Branch's North Fork. Next, after about ¼ mile, you come to the Thoreau Falls Trail on your left. This is your 5-mile return route south along North Fork into the East Branch valley. (The Ethan Pond Trail goes north through Zealand Notch to the Zealand Trail near AMC's Zealand Falls Hut.)

Take the Thoreau Falls Trail, left. It soon crosses North Fork above Thoreau Falls.

The series of cascades on your right was named, of course, for the author of *Walden*. This section of the trail,. before World War I, traversed burned land through which it was located by blazes on charred tree trunks. The fire had missed the forest below the falls; J. E. Henry began cutting that first-growth spruce in 1916.

Thoreau Falls and noontime lunch come together if the day's hike is proceeding on schedule. (You will have 7 miles, 4 hours, of afternoon walking back to Stillwater Junction.) When the North Fork is running full, the cascades glint and glimmer in the sun. The white water running over the ledges is visible to hikers on the western ridge, where Mount Bond, the highest summit in the area at 4,714 feet, extends north to Mount Guyot, and Zealand Ridge curves along the northern horizon.

Below Thoreau Falls, the trail keeps to North Fork's east bank as far as the crossing above Jumping Brook, which is about halfway down to the East Branch. Along here you walk on a haul road that leads to the railroad grade. The trail then follows the grade to another crossing. About 1¾ miles beyond this, you come to the East Branch and the bridge to the south bank. Then 15 minutes walking takes you to the Wilderness Trail at North Fork Junction.

Turn left onto the Wilderness Trail. You are heading east to Stillwater Junction, upstream

and somewhat more than 2 miles away. The trail offers the same good railroad-grade walking, except for the section near Crystal Brook, which J. E. Henry's surveyor bypassed in favor of the north bank. But the grade returns to the south bank beyond Crystal Brook and takes you to the next East Branch crossing soon after an opening in the woods that was Camp 18. Mount Carrigain appears ahead and to the right as you come to the river ledges before the last crossing to Stillwater Junction. With the completion of the day's loop hike, the time has come to decide on a campsite and put up the tent.

(Because the Carrigain Notch Trail from Stillwater to Camp 20 is less than 1 mile, there are several good campsites in the general area—Stillwater, Desolation Shelter, or Camp 20—it's a matter of individual choice. A night's tenting near Camp 20, where the Desolation Trail begins, means a direct start up Mount Carrigain on the third day.)

Third Day

Mount Carrigain via Desolation Trail and Signal Ridge Trail

Distance: 8 miles.
Walking time: 7 hours.

Leaving Stillwater Junction for Desolation Trail and Mount Carrigain, you take the Carrigain Notch Trail back past Desolation Shelter. The trail rises gradually, then makes a sharp left turn at the Camp 20 site. The Desolation Trail branches off straight across a small brook, which is the last water. You walk on your trip's final railroad grade; it was a spur track running from Camp 20 toward the mountain. From its end the trail follows and crosses between connecting logging roads up the ridge.

These former roads have thick bands of trees growing along them. Seen from a distance in the East Branch valley or from heights such as Mount Bond, they look like encircling, heavier-green, contour lines in the second-growth forest. Known to loggers as "dugway roads," these were literally dug into the mountainside to support heavy sled loads in

winter when teams hauled logs down to the railroad landings. The highest roads of J. E. Henry's operations were winter tracks using brush and side logs as "bunters" to keep the lighter sled loads from slipping off the steep slopes.

The Desolation Trail takes you to the end of the uppermost road, where the steepest ascent begins. This angle stopped J.E. Henry's logging not because it was difficult but because it was unprofitable. So, his shrewd assessment of cost saved the present virgin forest bordering Desolation Trail's top ½ mile to the summit. As a climber, you may also ponder the angle, but the slow upward pace will encourage you to enjoy the trees. The summit is 2 miles from Camp 20, wooded with low spruces, and overlooked by the tower.

The views on a clear day extend for miles in all directions. You can trace the route of your previous day's hike northwest of the summit. You look across the great country preserved in the Lincoln Woods Scenic Area. More distant mountains surround it. The

Franconias rise on the horizon to the west, and the Presidentials northeast. Mount Hancock is a near neighbor on the southwest, while, southward, Tripyramid and the Sandwich Range complete the circle.

Now the time has come to descend to where you started on the first day. You have 5 miles to go, and Signal Ridge will give you one more outlook.

The Signal Ridge Trail drops off the summit past the former fire lookout's cabin and well—which may have water in it. The trail continues the steep descent to Signal Ridge. There you bear left along the crest for a fine view across Carrigain Notch to the cliffs on Mount Lowell. After abrupt downward progress, the trail slabs through a logged valley, passes Carrigain Notch Trail coming in left, and goes on down to the Sawyer River Road and your parked car.

Mount Isolation

49. Mount Isolation

Time allowed: 3 days, 2 nights.
Distance (round trip): 14 miles.
Walking time: 11 hours.
Vertical rise: 3,200 feet.

A high ridge to separate you from the highway, a long wooded valley with a clear stream, two open-front shelters, and a remote, 4,005-foot peak south of Mount Washington—these all appear for your enjoyment on your way to the summit of Mount Isolation. You follow Rocky Branch Trail, Isolation Trail, and Davis Path on this undemanding, three-day hike. Because you return by the same route, you have the opportunity to see again the trees and brooks and views you passed hiking in; this double exposure reveals new secrets and discoveries.

First Day

NH 16 to Rocky Branch
Shelter Number 2

Distance: 3½ miles.
Walking time: 3 hours.

Drive north 5 miles on NH 16 from Jackson toward Pinkham Notch. At the edge of the White Mountain National Forest, you come to a small picnic area, right, beside the Ellis River. The Rocky Branch Trail begins

View from Mt. Isolation

near the top of the next rise, left (west) of the highway. Entering the woods a short distance before the trail sign, a section of old US 16 provides access to the trail and parking away from the present highway's traffic. Here you adjust your pack. (It should include a tent for use if the shelters are occupied.)

The trail takes you up west and north from the road into a forest of beech and yellow birch. You climb along two switchbacks, after which the trail swings west on a section relocated in 1971 to avoid a worn and washed out corner. Climbing steadily up this high Rocky Branch Ridge, you top a shoulder and follow an old logging road down a slight grade and across an area of springs that form Miles Brook. The trail ascends again. Spruce/fir woods begin at this elevation near the 3,000-foot sag in the main ridge, which attains 3,660 feet at an unnamed summit to the right of the trail. Across a moist height of land your boots squish in sphagnum moss and slip on the log corduroy that remains from its use for logging sleds.

You leave behind the taller evergreens as the country opens up into the Rocky Branch valley, and you look away to the Montalban Ridge with Mount Davis to the south and Mount Isolation to the north. The trail angles into young hardwoods and descends to Rocky Branch. There's no footbridge; you cross the stream on rocks to a ledge above pools. (This can be a dangerous crossing at high water.) Atop the bank beyond the ledge, the Isolation Trail begins on the right. (The Isolation Trail will be your upstream route on the second day.) Follow the Rocky Branch Trail sharply left a few yards to Rocky Branch Shelter Number 2 in a little clearing above the stream. This is a spacious board shelter, but popular, and you may have to set up your tent nearby.

Second Day

Rocky Branch Shelter Number 2
to Mount Isolation

Distance: 4½ miles.
Walking time: 3½ hours.

Your morning hike up Rocky Branch follows the Isolation Trail from the junction just north of Rocky Branch Shelter Number 2. The trail keeps to an old railroad grade much of the way. A forest of young white birches has taken over the blueberry slopes of forty years ago. Under the birches, hobble bushes spread broad leaves that shade the fern fronds and the fan-like leaves of wild sarsparilla. The valley has seen many changes: spruce logging, then the fires of 1914 and the scorched earth they brought, blueberry bushes, sprouting poplar and wild cherry growth, and now tall white birches where the old spruces grew.

The Isolation Trail lines up through the valley for about 1½ miles. In this distance the former logging railroad and the trail cross Rocky Branch several times. The log trestles are gone, and now you step from rock to rock, or wade. Occasional sections of the trail keep to the side-hill on the east bank for rough but somewhat dryer footing above the stream. Large boulders here and there interrupt the flowing water and form pools below alder thickets. You walk in a long grove of white birches.

Beyond the final crossing to the west bank, the trail leads into spruces and over damp ground along a tributary brook. After 1 mile, you reach the source at the water supply for Isolation Shelter. Rocks cup this spring, which flows over a concrete spout. The trail jogs right then left up a steep bank and over it, then soon descends to the log shelter, elevation 3,757 feet, and popular.

Isolation Shelter's open gable end eliminates the overhanging eaves more common on open-front shelters. You don't duck down to enter. Upper and lower bunks accommodate eight or ten hikers. The log walls, the big rock in front, the fireplace against it, and the surrounding green spruce and fir trees, all suggest a simpler and more primitive time in the mountains. You may think back even to the days when the great-grandfathers of the present young male hikers similarly sported moustaches and beards. Comparison, however, ends with this fashion. Great-grandfathers wore cowhide boots and ate fried salt pork and trout; now progress has brought Vibram soles and freeze-dried beef stroganoff.

Clear skies at Isolation Shelter this second day of your trip mean that you eat a quick lunch and head for Mount Isolation. If rain is falling you'll want to postpone the climb until morning. Mount Isolation is only ¾ mile south on the Davis Path. This trail runs left and right (south and north) past the shelter's west end. Turn left onto the Davis Path.

The Isolation Trail coincides with the Davis Path for a few yards, then forks right. (The Isolation Trail descends into Dry River valley and terminates at the Dry River Trail near Dry River Shelter Num-

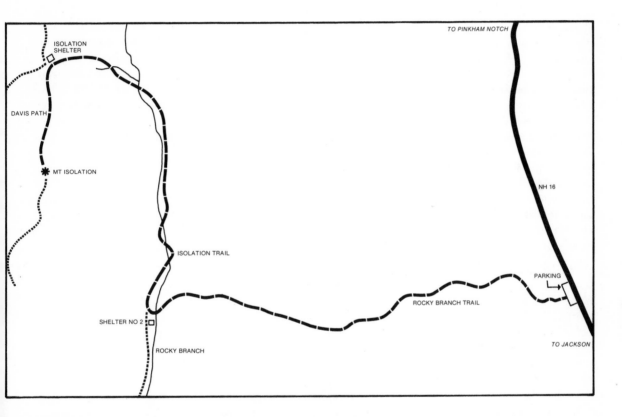

ber 2. The Davis Path extends from Notchland in Crawford Notch, at US 302, to Mount Washington.)

Stay on the Davis Path. It climbs a spruce ridge overlooking Rocky Branch valley, left. But keep your eye on the trail. Watch for a spur trail right, at a small cairn. It takes you scrambling up through spruce scrub to the flat rocky summit of Mount Isolation.

The spruce scrub offers no obstacle to the outlook as you step across the ledges. The western horizon at once draws and holds your attention. The southern peaks of the Presidential Range begin in the south near Crawford Notch at Mount Jackson and extend north to Clinton, Eisenhower, Franklin, and Monroe, in a long serrated array to the great peak of Washington, which strikes into the sky four miles north of you. Mount Isolation places you high between two valleys that sweep down from Mount Washington to Crawford Notch; the line of summits, near whose northern end you

Mount Isolation

stand, is named Montalban Ridge. You have hiked the valley to the east, Rocky Branch; to the west between you and the southern peaks, you look into Dry River valley, which isn't dry. Its upper waters are apparent as cascades on the headwall of Oakes Gulf between you and Mounts Monroe and Washington. (Dry River can quickly become a raging torrent. It bears another, more appropriate name: Mount Washington River.)

Mount Isolation is a grandstand seat for cloud shows. Often, white wisps and tumbling fogs swirl among the southern peaks. On some bright, clear days, storm clouds suddenly mass around Washington's cone and obscure the buildings and towers. If the storm threatens rain on Mount Isolation, retreat to the shelter. Retrace your way east down the spur trail and turn left onto the Davis Path for the shelter 20 minutes away.

Third Day

Isolation Shelter to NH 16

Distance: 6 miles.
Walking time: 4½ hours.

Perhaps this morning brings clear skies after a previous rainy afternoon that kept you from Mount Isolation. You still have time to go up it, because this third day's hike is almost as moderate as the previous days; you have 6 miles ahead, about 4½ hours of walking time.

If you're early enough to Mount Isolation, you'll see the sunrise brightening Mount Washington, or maybe a shining white cloud around the peak. If rain pours down this morning, and you really want to reach the summit, you'll just have to slog along through the downpour. You'd be wiser to wait for another chance; turning back short of the summit is part of mountain climbing. And there's nothing to see on Mount Isolation in a rainstorm except spruce scrub, ledges, Labrador tea, and mountain cranberry.

For the return hike from Isolation Shelter, walk back east on the Isolation Trail to Rocky Branch, and down the stream to the junction with the Rocky Branch Trail. Turn left onto the Rocky Branch Trail, cross the stream, and climb over the ridge. Then it's all downhill to NH 16 and your car.

Mount Isolation

50. The Mahoosuc Range

Time allowed: 7 days, 6 nights.
Distance: 29 miles.
Walking time: 31 hours.
Vertical rise: 8,500 feet.*

The northeastward distance from Gorham, New Hampshire, to Grafton Notch, Maine, is only 18 miles "as the crow flies" but stretches to a rugged, curving 29 miles when you hike the AMC's Mahoosuc Trail. Allowing for a southerly swing and for zigzags from peak to peak, those extra 11 miles are up and down.

The varied worlds along the way include hardwood forests, mountain meadows, spruce-shaded slopes, subarctic barrens, frequent ledges, sharp ravines, and summit after summit. The Mahoosucs are a a unique experience. Leisurely travel enhances the experience; the Mahoosucs deserve a week. Of the 7 days alloted, you hike 6 days with time to relax at intervals and still make camp long before dark. One day is a spare. Use it when a storm engulfs the range by taking refuge in a tent or in one of the four log shelters. If your week's weather turns out to be perfect, you have a day to rest and loaf at Speck Pond's

* This is an estimate based on map contour counting; the rises are frequent.

shelter before completing the Mahoosuc Range on Old Speck Mountain and descending to Grafton Notch, where you meet asphalt again on Me 26.

Transportation arrangements will vary to fit individual plans. You can leave your car parked near the trail at Grafton Notch, off Me 26, and be driven around west to Gorham; or you may plan to be met at Grafton Notch on the seventh day.

Although either Gorham or Grafton Notch could be the starting point, the northeast direction from Gorham has three specific advantages. First, you don't face Old Speck from Grafton Notch with a full pack; the trail is said to be the steepest 1½ miles in the mountains. Second, from Gorham you easily climb Mount Hayes and Cascade Mountain, the first two summits, and on each you are treated to superb views of the Presidential Range's northern peaks and Mount Washington. Third, the progress northeastward gives you an exciting sense of increasing wildness. With this you also enjoy a continual, although intermittent, ascent: Mount Hayes, 2,566 feet; Mount Success, 3,590 feet;

Old Speck, 4,180 feet; with ten other summits in between.

As you travel northeastward you leave behind the White Mountains proper, and with them, tourism. You also leave behind civilization and industry, although you will be reminded of these for a day or so: the stench from Berlin's paper mills and the polluted Androscoggin River accompanies you when the wind is from the west.

First Day

NH 16 to Mount Hayes to Hayes-Cascade Col

Distance: 4¼ miles.
Walking time: 4 hours.

You have time to drive by car in the morning and climb in the afternoon.

Start walking at the railroad bridge 1 mile north of Gorham and east of NH 16 between Gorham and Berlin. Under the black steel structure, a wooden ramp and footbridge take you across the Androscoggin River. On the far bank, turn right onto a dirt road for the ½ mile to the

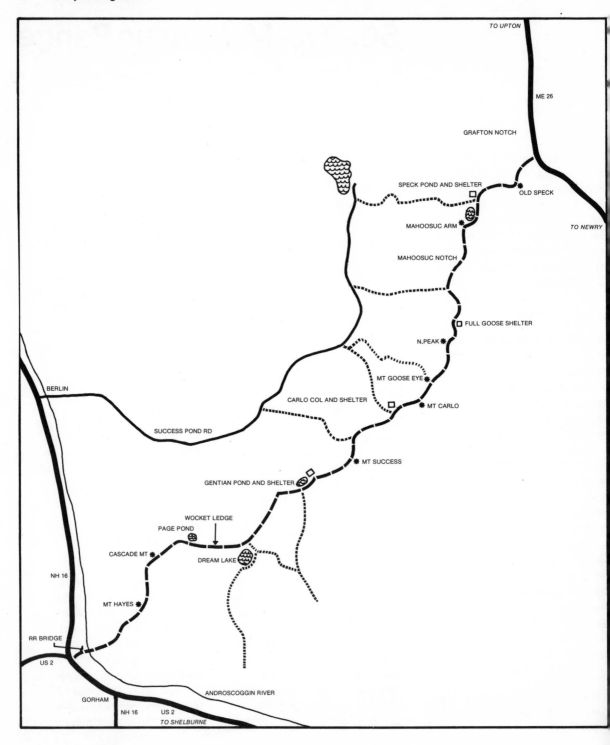

The Mahoosuc Range

powerhouse and canal. Cross the canal by the upper level of the powerhouse, and make for the woods beyond the canal bank east of the dam. The Mahoosuc Trail leads north up the canal, then bears right, climbing to a power line, the path of which it crosses at an ascending angle. You enter logged areas where the trail is marked by yellow paint. Pass a spur trail right. (It leads to the Mount Hayes cliffs and Mascot Pond.) Keeping to the main trail and crossing a small brook, you ascend more steeply and come to Popsy Spring on the left. This water provides refreshment for the short climb to Mount Hayes's rocky summit.

The view includes the big bend of the Androscoggin River west and south around Mount Hayes's base. High in the west the outlines that cut the sky are Mount Madison, Mount Adams, and Mount Washington. Southward, the Carter-Moriah Range forms the eastern wall of Pinkham Notch. At sunset, the Presidential peaks glow pink, while on their eastern slopes purple shadows extend into the valley.

You begin to think of darkness, and you still have a ½-hour hike to water in the col between Mount Hayes and Cascade Mountain.

The Mahoosuc Trail leaves Mount Hayes's summit east through blueberry bushes, spruces, and ledges. Follow it down into hardwoods and broad-leaved hobble bushes. The col between Hayes and Cascade might better be described with the woodsman's term, "sag," rather than the mountaineer's "col"; it's a low wooded valley between two mountains. The water, mostly to the right of the trail at the lowest point in the col, collects in shallow forest pools.

You must dip a cup to fill a cooking pot or plastic folding pail. Searching farther up the slope, you find a relatively level place to set up your tent. (The plan of this hike takes you to a shelter for each of the next five nights. You may need your tent, however, in case the shelters are occupied. Or, if you like, you may use the tent later in the week for camping between shelters. In the latter case, make

sure you carry enough water; it's scarce along the trail.

Here in the col, as night settles over the mountains, contrasting sounds remind you that you're between civilization and the wild. The Berlin mills roar steadily in the valley to the north, and on up Cascade Mountain a moose bellows out a sound like an old farm dinner horn: OOOOWNN-AAHHHHHHNNHH! It's an absurd yet spine-tingling call, which rouses you from your sleeping bag and has you sitting up to stare out into the moonlit woods.

Second Day
Hayes-Cascade Col to Gentian Pond Shelter

Distance: 7 miles.
Walking time: 6 hours.

In the morning, you shoulder your pack and climb Cascade Mountain through beech woods, which change to small, park-like maples, then to bushes and broken slabs of rock. If you're early enough on Cascade Mountain's summit ledges on a clear day, you'll be treated to a special sun-

The Mahoosuc Range

rise show. The Androscoggin valley often lies deeply hidden in white fog. You stand far above and look across to the Presidentials shining in the new day's sun.

Beyond Cascade Mountain, you hike along the ridge through spruce woods alternating with ledges and damp sphagnum moss. Stumps show old forest-fire charring. At the east shoulder, the Mahoosuc Trail drops steeply toward a view of distant peaks, crags, and forested ridges. Ahead you may see ravens soaring and barking over the rocky peaks known as the Trident. The descent pushes your pack against your shoulders, and your hands seek steadying holds on bushes and trees, until the trail levels out at Trident col.

A spur trail leads left to water and the site of the former Trident Shelter. (Strong back-packers with 6 hours of time often camp the first night here, about 6½ miles from NH 16.)

The Mahoosuc Trail leads on eastward by an old logging road, descending some-what and slabbing south of the middle Trident Peak. You cross a trickle of water here and there through the hard-woods. The trail takes you up to a more recent, bulldozed road, which, after a short distance, bears right. The trail branches left, and you fol-low it among bushes and young trees up a gradual slope to a level section. The approach to Page Pond through tall grass shows you first the spruce ridge beyond, then the oval of water. In late summer-time, closed gentians bloom near the beaver dam. Depend-ing on the latest beaver work, the trail may cross over the dam's poles and mud.

An easy walk among spruces brings you to the base of the next height, Wocket Ledge, where the ridge rears up sud-denly. You dig for footholds and test spruce roots and branches for secure hand grips. The ledge itself appears at the crest 50 yards to the left, about ¾ mile from Page Pond. The climb has been strenuous, and you'll want to sit for a while and look off at the wild country near and far.

Back to the trail and up be-yond the open ledge, you follow the trail in spruces. Descend-ing, you pass a spring and the beginning of a Peabody Brook branch. Ascending and descend-ing— the theme of the Ma-hoosucs,—you slant down to a mountain pond called Dream Lake.

The trail turns left along the lake shore. By stepping quietly through bushes down to the water, perhaps you see a moose feeding, belly-deep in the lake. If only lily pads and quiet ripples meet your eyes, pro-ceed along the trail and across the inlet to the northeast end. There the Peabody Brook Trail terminates at the Ma-hoosuc Trail. (The Peabody Brook Trail comes up from North Road in Shelburne off US 2.) A short walk down Peabody Brook Trail takes you to a striking camera shot across Dream Lake to Mount Washington.

Returning to the Mahoosuc Trail, which, from here on, coincides with the Appalachian Trail, you head east for about 1 mile across a height of land so flat and swampy as to be almost imperceptible. The new watershed's first display appears at Moss Pond. As you hike along the pond to the end, you see on your right a beaver dam that seems barely to hold the brimming little basin from pouring down the mountainside. The trail follows the outlet brook, turns right, and plunges down through ledges, tumbled rocks, and tree roots, to Gentian Pond.

At Gentian Pond the trail follows the rough shoreline to the south ledges. Here a gap in the rock carries away the outlet water. Bark-skinned poles, which represent earlier beaver meals, form a miniature log jam. The gap in the ledges separates you from Gentian Pond Shelter on its rock perch a stone's throw away. The distance is actually minor, but it's often been described in appropriately unflattering terms after a hard day's hike. Easing down carefully or detouring around, you must make a final scramble to the shelter. (From Gentian Pond Shelter, the Austin Brook Trail drops down to Shelburne's North Road. This is the last official trail south from the Mahoosuc Trail.)

The pond water is handy and serves well enough to rinse yourself—but for drinking water you follow a faint path north among the shore spruces to an inlet trickling clear and cold past green sphagnum moss. The sign by the shelter once listed the distance as 100 yards, to which a doubting hiker had added in pencil another zero.

The shelter is worth the scramble to get to it. Built of logs, with its open front facing a fireplace's piled stones and a faraway view into the Androscoggin valley, it is an ideal place to enjoy the spectacular late afternoon sunlight and evening shadows across the valley. Sometimes the peaks in the Carter Range remain lighted for a time before darkening, and a plane catches the sunlight higher in the sky, where it appears to you as an illusion without meaning or mission. Down in the valley, car lights blink along US 2. But by then your campfire gives you a special personal light.

Third Day
Gentian Pond Shelter to
Carlo Col Shelter

Distance: 5¾ miles.
Walking time: 6½ hours.

Mount Success is your big objective after breakfast at Gentian Pond Shelter. The climb measures the mountain's bulk rather than its height, which is a moderate 3,590 feet. The up-and-down approach makes you think that the mountain has retreated beyond ridges to fortify itself against your attack.

In early morning, a steep climb places you on ledges above the pond. Then you descend and climb again over the first of two rugged little hills protruding from the mountainside. After the second knob, a little rivulet provides a canteen filling: no more certain water until the end of the day's hike at Carlo Col Shelter.

The trail continues, steep and difficult. You surmount blocks of granite, which obstruct the way and indicate an old slide. Then you cross a washout grown to brush, and begin to climb in the spruce/fir forest.

The Mahoosuc Range

The damp woods are the habitat of the deliberate spruce grouse. The trees dwindle to evergreen scrub at open ledges, and you climb toward the summit through more scrub and over bare rock.

Mount Success spreads before you northern vistas of lakes and wilderness as well as an unusual perspective toward the Presidentials. The summit itself presents the first muddy areas typical of high Mahoosuc ridges above treeline. Lying in hollows between rock faces, the black earth has a dry crust in hot weather; the crust covers the muck and lures you into ankle-deep organic soup.

Various heath plants border this rich humus. Matted dwarf spruces testify to the severe winds.

(There is a former salvage trail leading to Shelburne from the wreckage of a DC-3 that crashed on the southwest shoulder in 1954. New spruce growth has made the site difficult to find, and the salvage trail has grown to bushes.)

From Mount Success, the Mahoosuc Trail turns left down barren shoulders and through scrub for ½ mile and then into the woods. You pass the Success Trail left. (The Success Trail is the first of five trails to Success Pond Road from the Mahoosuc Trail. It leads down to the Brown Company's Success Pond Road, which runs northeast fourteen miles from Berlin.)

For the next 2 miles, the Mahoosuc Trail follows a northeast ridge. You climb and slab wooded contours, then descend, only to climb again. An Appalachian Trail sign marks the New Hampshire–Maine line. The immediate challenge in Maine turns out to be two ravines that resemble abandoned rock quarries. Situated on two small cols along the ridge and separated by a short, yet vigorous ascent, the ravines are a fitting conclusion to a day on Mount Success.

The final climb down the ledge to Carlo col gives any cautious backpacker pause for thought. You may wisely decide to take off your pack and lower it to a companion who has made his way down, packless, by clinging to spruces. A few yards beyond the ledge, the Carlo Col Trail comes in from the Success Pond Road. Turn left onto the Carlo Col Trail and follow it down a stony ¼ mile. At the first sure water, which you'll notice because you're walking in it, keep watch for a spur trail, right, up a steep short bank. It leads to Carlo Col Shelter. A sign so informs you, but on a rainy afternoon with fog you might walk by.

Fourth Day
Carlo Col Shelter to
Full Goose Shelter

Distance; 4½ miles.
Walking time: 4 hours.

This day's hike features Mount Goose Eye and barren ridges such as you might see in Labrador. It begins with a cool, starting climb from Carlo Col Shelter back to the Mahoosuc Trail. You'll feel the morning coolness because the shelter is 3,000 feet high. Turn left from the Carlo Col Trail onto the Mahoosuc Trail. Mount Carlo, elevation 3,562, rises ahead, and the trail leads up through spruces. After a night's rain the branches can be wet and cold. But the climb warms you before you emerge on Mount Carlo's bare summit. Perhaps the wide views lie hidden in morning mists or gathering clouds.

The trail crosses into the spruce woods, through which it leads you downhill to a sloping meadow. Water sometimes gathers there in small pools. Many variations of these tundra-like meadows occur between here and Old Speck; they become part of the changing Mahoosuc scene. The steep drop from the meadow to a col presents you at once with the next climb: Mount Goose Eye.

Legend gives this mountain's early name as "Goose High," because the summit was an obstacle to migrating geese. If so, the geese had to clear by a few wingbeats a rocky 3,860-foot mass.

As you approach Mount Goose Eye, the Mahoosuc Trail offers several ledges and small cliffs. These give you a chance to experiment with toehold climbing as you test by hand the tensile strength of brush in-

securely rooted in rock. The trail continues steeply enough to take you up 500 feet in about ¼ mile, to a bare shoulder east of the summit. (Branching left, the Goose Eye Trail leads over the summit and down to the Success Pond Road.)

The Mahoosuc Trail turns abruptly right, away from the summit, and runs along a bare ridge through scattered small spruces, downward to the next rise over East Peak. On the open sections here, cairns mark the trail or worn turf indicates the route. Evergreen scrub alternates with barren areas. You come to a left turn, north, and down, from East Peak. Across an open slope, cairns and wandering paths lead toward the eastern end of this great slanting meadow. The nearby subarctic scene reveals northern forests and lakes in the distance.

You pick up the trail where it drops through scrub to the col. You head for Goose Eye's North Peak through more open land and spruces. At a damp wooded ravine, you come upon small pools of water cupped in sphagnum moss. If the moss

has absorbed all the water, a handful squeezed above a cup produces a drink.

North Peak is steep, too. The wide barrens resemble treeline areas in the Presidentials and Franconias, although here vegetation extends to the highest ground. Much of the rock is crumbly and soft. Gravel in the trail crunches under your boots.

Sunny weather attracts birds. They leave the barrens in storms and rain, or take shelter under the flattened evergreens. By late summer, juncos and white-throated sparrows remain, usually in the lower growth. Below the barrens, in spruce/fir woods, you see both the black-capped chickadee and the boreal chickadee. The boreals are ridiculously inquisitive. They flit nearby as you rest, and they comment in a series of notes deeper and shorter than those of the black-capped.

On high meadows and barrens, the spruces are often flattened against the ground. Taller, more protected trees show effects of the prevailing northwest winds, for they lean away from that quarter and put out longer branches on the leeward side. The ridges take the full force of storms bearing down from the forested north country; there's almost no protection between the Mahoosucs and the storm factories up in Canada. Clouds and rain often settle over the range, and winds are icy. If you must brave a drenching exposure on a ridge such as Goose Eye's North Peak, you face subarctic winds and temperatures.

From North Peak, the Mahoosuc Trail continues east along open ground beyond the summit. You follow and descend through scrub and barrens into head-high spruces. You find yourself walking down over ledges among older trees. Another mountain looms before you. The trail seems to vanish, however, at a wall of brush, and you are hemmed in by a small ledge on your right.

Face the ledge and pull yourself up. You emerge by Full Goose Shelter where you'll spend the night. It opens toward Fulling Mill Mountain and the precipitous valleys

of Bull Branch and Goose Eye Brook. Beyond are the mountains that rise above and conceal Grafton Notch.

For a drink of water, walk past the front of the shelter and take the steep path down to the spring.

Fifth Day

Full Goose Shelter to Speck Pond Shelter

Distance: 5 miles.
Walking time: 7 hours.

The Mahoosuc Trail continues east from Full Goose Shelter by dropping down the overlook in front of the shelter, to a ravine that is only an infinitesimal hint of the Mahoosuc Notch to come. But first, Fulling Mill Mountain. You climb up a steady grade through evergreens and reach a meadow between two wooded summits. The trail turns left and you rapidly descend, in trees again, 1,000 feet to the western end of Mahoosuc Notch. (At a junction, left, the Notch Trail comes in from the Success Pond Road.)

You turn sharply right and follow the Mahoosuc Trail down a pleasant slope among spruces at 2,500 feet elevation. You are entering Mahoosuc Notch. The gentle approach leaves you unprepared for the gigantic rock slabs and chunks, which seem to have fallen from the high cliffs on either side. But they have not fallen recently; they are draped with moss and crusted with lichens.

The moss forms treacherous pads over crevices and caves. Be careful not to step on any moss that reaches from slab to slab. As you crawl under overhanging rocks, you hear water trickling deep down in caves. Winter chill comes to you from the ice caverns. You follow white paint marks as the trail twists and turns for 1 mile among the rocks. You should plan on at least 2 hours during which you'll be busy reaching for handholds, stepping wide, balancing, and creeping.

At the Notch's eastern end, you resume normal woods hiking. The trail follows the brook past a beaver pond. Below this, after entering big hardwoods, you turn left away from the brook, climb up a short distance, and bear right onto an old logging road. In a slabbing ascent, the trail rounds Mahoosuc Mountain.

The trail follows a logging road toward a sag known as Notch 2, until you cross a brook. After a rough section, you begin the day's second real climb as the trail swings up Mahoosuc Arm. Much of the way, the trail rises among tall, old spruces. Mahoosuc Arm extends 1,200 feet above Mahoosuc Notch. About halfway, or ¾ mile from the Notch, you come to a seasonal brook in a rock sluice; don't count on water.

Climbing on, you enter evergreen scrub and begin to ascend sloping ledges. The trail follows cairns along rock worn by glaciers and ages of weathering. You come out on the bare ridge itself, Mahoosuc Arm, which is really a mountain almost 3,800 feet high. It displays the same low vegetation that you saw on North Peak. Here, dwarf tamarack lies flat against rooted turf and gravel. On a cold and stormy day as you walk across this windswept barren, you may find yourself shivering, less adapted to the environment than the plants.

A big cairn and post on the open ledges mark the summit of Mahoosuc Arm. Here the Mahoosuc Trail turns right. (A cutoff trail to Speck Pond Trail forks left.) The Mahoosuc Trail jogs approximately south and then north along the ridge and enters occasional scrub between open meadows. Now going down more steeply through spruce woods, you descend to 3,500 feet and Speck Pond. The trail circles to the east shore, and at the upper end you come to Speck Pond Shelter. A deep, little mountain lake, Speck Pond reflects the surrounding pointed spruces, or sometimes, due to its elevation, lies smothered in clouds. (The Speck Pond Trail leaves from the shelter for the Success Pond Road.)

Sixth Day

Allowed for bad weather or to spend at Speck Pond

Seventh Day

Speck Pond Shelter to Grafton Notch

Distance: 2¾ miles.
Walking time: 3½ hours.

Your departure in the morning should be adjusted to the weather. Foggy daylight and gloomy spruce woods have been known to brighten in an hour, and too-eager hikers have looked back from Grafton Notch to the sunlit summit of Old Speck, which they left shrouded in clouds. Now that you have been conditioned by the Mahoosucs, you should be able to climb Old Speck and descend to Grafton Notch in 3½ hours. So wait awhile for clear skies.

Take the Mahoosuc Trail from Speck Pond Shelter northeast. Directly, it climbs a large knoll, drops down, and then up and around another ridge. In the next little valley, you pass a spring east of the trail. You begin to climb up Old Speck along ledges that lead you on by their angle and by the line of the crest rather than by any cairns or signs, which are mostly absent. Keep heading up.

The Mahoosuc Range

This rocky shoulder joins spruce woods, and the trail, bearing right, leads into them. The trail parallels for a time the blue paint blazes identifying the boundary of Grafton Notch State Park. You are nearing the end of the Mahoosuc Trail. It soon meets the Old Speck Trail from Grafton Notch and the highway, Me 26. (The Old Speck Trail was formerly the Fire-Warden's Trail. On your left also, the Old Speck Link Trail joins. It's an alternate for the upper ½ mile of the Old Speck Trail.) Turn right onto the Old Speck Trail. Follow it a short distance to Old Speck's summit. The level clearing in the spruces centers on the unused tower's steel framework. For views, an eastern path to open rocks, known as East Spur, gives a clear outlook toward the Rangeley Lakes, where on a sunny day the waters shine like mirrors.

From the summit clearing on Old Speck, retrace your steps along the Old Speck Trail and pass the left turn into the Mahoosuc Trail. You come to ledges and a brief vista through the spruces. Then the Old Speck Trail takes you down the steepest descent you're likely to make in some time. The trail falls away 2,700 feet in 1½ miles. It's a gash in the spruce/fir woods, and it's lined with stones and gravel. Part way down this section, you come to a pool of cold water under a rock on the left.

At the fire-warden's abandoned cabin, the trail crosses a little brook. (The East Spur Trail leaves on the right. The Old Speck Link Trail joins left.) Keep straight past the cabin. The evergreens give way to yellow birch, beech, and other deciduous trees, because the rapidly lowering altitude creates a milder climate. The trail in wet weather becomes a muddy flume; then you engage in 1 mile of heel digging and taking to the bushes for more secure footing. The last 100 yards to the Grafton Notch Highway (Me 26) are level. Here the Old Speck Trail ends. (The Appalachian Trail, which has been coinciding with it, follows the blacktop highway, north, ½ mile to the Baldpate Mountain Trail, right. The Grafton Notch Shelter is ¼ mile east on this trail.) You hear cars for the first time in a week.

Camping in the Mahoosucs

The Mahoosuc Range

Photographs on pages 40, 44,
70, 92, and 150 are by Daniel Doan.
All other photographs are by
Fred Bavendam.

Maps are by Michael Sheppard.